# Bear Brownie

## by H. P. Robinson

From Animal Autobiographies by H. P. Robinson

REVISED BY JANE FIELDING

NEW YORK A. L. CHATTERTON CO.

# CHAPTER I.

## HOW I TUMBLED DOWNHILL.

It is not easy for one to believe that he ever was a cub. Of course, I know that I was, and as it was only nine years ago I ought to remember it fairly clearly.

It is not so much a mere matter of size, although it is doubtful if any young bear realizes how small he is. My father and mother seemed enormous to me, but, on the other hand, my sister was smaller than I, and perhaps the fact that I could always box her ears when I wanted to gave me an exaggerated idea of my own importance. Not that I did it very often, except when she used to bite my hind-toes. Every bear, of course, likes to chew his own feet, for it is one of the most soothing and comforting things in the world; but it is horrid to have anyone else come up behind you when you are asleep, and begin to chew your feet for you. And that was Kahwa--that was my sister, my name being Brownie--was always doing, and I simply had to slap her well whenever she did.

But, as I said, cubhood is not a matter of size only. As I look down at this glossy coat of mine, it is hard to believe that it was ever a dirty yellow color, and all ridiculous wool and fluff, as young cubs' coats are. But I must have been fluffy, because I remember how my mother, after she had been licking me for any length of time, used to be obliged to stop and wipe the fur out of her mouth with the back of her paw. Every time my mother had to wipe her mouth she used to try to box my ears, so that when she stopped licking me, I, knowing what was coming next, would tuck my head down as far as it would go between my legs, and keep it there till she began licking again.

Yes, when I stop to think, I know, from many things, that I must have been just an ordinary cub. For instance, my very earliest recollection is of tumbling downhill.

Like all bears, I was born and lived on the hillside. In the Rocky Mountains, where my home was, there is nothing but hills, or mountains, for miles and miles, so that you can wander on for day after day, always going up one side of a hill and down the other, and up and down again; and at the bottom of almost every valley there is a stream or river, which for most of the year swirls along nosily and full of water.

In the winter the whole country is covered with snow many feet deep, which, as it falls, slides off the hillsides, and is drifted by the winds into the valleys and hollows till the smaller ones are filled up nearly to the tops of the trees. But bears do not see much of that, for when the first snow comes we get into our dens and go half asleep, and stay hibernating till springtime. And you have no idea how delightful hibernating is, nor how excruciatingly stiff we are when we wake up, and how hungry!

The snow lies over everything for months, until in the early spring the warm west winds begin to blow, melting the snow from one side of the mountains. Then the sun grows hotter and hotter day by day, and helps to melt it until most of the mountain slopes are clear; but in sheltered places and in the bottoms of the little hollows the snow stays in patches till far into the summer. We bears comes out from our winter sleep when the snow is not quite gone, when the whole earth everywhere is still wet with it, and the streams, swollen with floods, are bubbling and boiling along so that the air is filled with the noise of them by night and day.

Our home was well up one of the hillsides, where two huge cedar-trees shot up side by side close by a jutting mass of rock. In between the roots of the trees and under the rock was as good a house as a family of bears could want--roomy enough for all four of us, perfectly sheltered, and hidden and dry. Can you imagine how warm and comfy it was when we were all snuggled in there, with our arms round each other, and our faces buried in each other's fur? Anyone looking in would have seen nothing but a huge ball of brown fluff.

It was from just outside the door that I tumbled downhill.

It must have been early in the year, because the ground was still very wet and soft, and the gully at the bottom full of snow. Of course, if I had not been a cub I should never have fallen, for big bears do not tumble downhill. If by any chance anything did start one, and he found he could not stop himself, he would know enough to tuck in his head and paws out of harm's way; but I only knew that somehow, in romping with Kahwa, I had lost my balance, and was going-- goodness knew where! I went all spread out like a squirrel, first on my head, then on my back, then on my tummy, clutching at everything that I passed, slapping the ground with my outstretched paws, and squealing for help. Bump! bang! slap! bump! I went, hitting trees and thumping all the wind out of me against the earth, and at last--souse into the snow!

Wow-ugh! How cold and wet it was! And it was deep--so deep, indeed, that I was buried completely out of sight; and I doubt if I should ever have got out alive had not my mother come down and dug me out with her nose and paws. Then she half pushed and half smacked me uphill again, and when I got home I was the wettest, coldest, sorest, wretchedest bear-cub in the Rocky Mountains.

Then, while I lay and whimpered, my mother spent the rest of the day licking me into the semblance of a respectable bearskin again. But I was bruised and nervous for days afterwards.

That tumble of mine gave us the idea of the game which Kahwa and I used to play almost every day after that. Kahwa would take her stand with her back against the rock by our door, just at the point where the hill went off most steeply, and it was my business to come charging up the hill at her and try to pull her down. What fun it was! Sometimes I was the one to stand against the rock, and Kahwa tried to pull me down. She could not do it; but she was plucky, and used to come at me so ferociously that I often wondered for a minute whether it was only play or whether she was really angry.

Best of all was when mother used to play with us. Then she put her back to the rock, and we both attacked her at once from opposite sides, each trying to get hold of a hind-leg just above the foot. If she put her head down to pretend to bite either of us, the other jumped for her ear. Sometimes we would each get hold of an ear, and hang on as hard as we could, while she pretended we were hurting her dreadfully, growling and shaking her head, and making as much fuss as she could; but if in our excitement either of us did chance to bite a little too hard, we always knew it. With a couple of cuffs, hard enough to make us yelp, she would throw us to one side and the other, and there was no more play for that day. And mother could hit hard when she liked. I have seen her smack father in a way that would have broken all the bones in a cub's body, and killed any human being outright.

But to Kahwa and me both father and mother were very gentle and kind in those first helpless days, and I suppose they never punished us unless we deserved it. Later on my father and I had differences, as you will hear. But in that first summer our lives, uneventful, were happy.

CHAPTER II.

CUBHOOD DAYS.

When they are small, bear-cubs rarely go about alone. The whole family usually keeps together, or, if it separates, it is generally into couples--one cub with each of the parents; or the father goes off alone, leaving both cubs with the mother. A cub toddling off alone in its own woolly, comfortable ignorance would be sure to make all manner of mistakes in what it ate, and it might find itself in very serious trouble in other ways.

Bears, when they live far enough away from man, have absolutely nothing to be afraid of. There are, of course, bigger bears--perhaps bigger ones of our own kind, either black or brown ("cinnamon," the brown members of our family are called), or, especially, grizzly. But I never heard of a grizzly bear hurting one of us. When I smell a grizzly in the neighborhood, I confess that it seems wiser to go round the other side of the hill; but that is probably inherited superstition more than anything else. My father and mother did it, and so do I. Apart from these, there lives nothing in the forest that a full-grown bear has any cause to fear. He goes where he pleases and does what he likes, and nobody ventures to dispute his rights. With a cub, however, it is different.

I had heard my father and mother speak of pumas, or mountain lions, and I knew their smell well enough--and did not like it. But I shall never forget the first one that I saw.

We were out together--father, mother, Kahwa and I--and it was getting well on in the morning. The sun was up, and the day growing warm, and I, wandering drowsily along with my nose to the ground, had somehow strayed away from the rest, when suddenly I smelled puma very strong. As I threw myself up on my haunches, he came out from behind a tree, and stood facing me only a few yards away. I was simply paralyzed with fear--one of the two or three times in my life when I have been honestly and thoroughly frightened. As I looked at him, wondering what would happen next, he crouched down till he was almost flat along the ground, and I can see him now, his whole yellow body almost hidden behind his head, his eyes blazing, and his tail going slap, slap from side to side. How I wished that I had a tail!

Then inch by inch he crept towards me, very slowly, putting one foot forward and then the other. I did not know what to do, and so did what proved to be the best thing possible: I sat quite still, and screamed for mother as loud as I could. She must have known from my voice that something serious was the matter, because in a second, just as the puma's muscles were growing tense for the final spring, there was a sudden crash of broken boughs behind me, a feeling as if a whirlwind was going by, and my mother shot past me straight at the puma. I had no idea that she could go so fast. The puma was up on his hind-legs to meet her, but her impetus was so terrific that it bore him backwards, without seeming to check her speed in the least, and away they went rolling over and over down the hill.

But it was not much of a fight. The puma, willing enough to attack a little cub like me, knew that he was no match for my mother, and while they were still rolling he wrenched himself loose, and was off among the trees like a shadow.

When mother came back to me blood was running over her face, where at the moment of meeting, the puma had managed to give her one wicked, tearing claw down the side of her nose. So, as soon as my father and Kahwa joined us, we all went down to the stream, where mother bathed her face, and kept it in the cold water for nearly the whole day.

It was probably in some measure to pay me out for this scrape, and to give me another lesson in the unwisdom of too much independence and inquisitiveness in a youngster, that my parents, soon after this sad event, allowed me to get into trouble with that porcupine.

One evening my father had taken us to a place where the ground was full of mountain lilies. It was early in the year, when the green shoots were just beginning to appear above the earth; and wherever there was a shoot there was a bulb down below. And a mountain lily bulb is one of the very nicest things to eat that there is--so sweet, and juicy, and crisp! The place was some distance from our home, and after that first visit Kahwa and I kept begging to be taken there again. At last my father yielded, and we set out early one morning just before day was breaking.

We were not loitering on the way, but trotting steadily along all together, and Kahwa and I, at least, were full of expectation of the lily bulbs in store, when in a little open space among the trees, we came upon an object unlike anything I had ever seen before. As we came upon it, I could have declared that it was moving--then that it was an animal which, at sight of us, had stopped stock still, and tucked its head and toes in underneath it. But it certainly was not moving now, and did not look as if it ever could move again, so finally I concluded that it must be a large fungus or a strange new kind of hillock, with black and white grass growing all over it. My father and mother had stopped short when they saw it, and just sat up on their haunches and looked at it; and Kahwa did the same, snuggling up close to my mother's side. Was it an animal, or a fungus, or only a mound of earth? The way to find out was to smell it. So, without any idea of hurting it, I trotted up and reached out my nose. As I did so it shrank a little more into itself, and became rounder and more like a fungus than ever; but the act of shrinking also made the black and white grass stick out a little farther, so that my nose met it sooner than I expected, and I found that, if it was grass, it was very sharp grass, and pricked horribly. I tried again, and again it shrank up and pricked me worse than ever. Then I heard my father chuckling to himself.

That made me angry, for I always have detested being laughed at, and, without stopping to think, I smacked the thing just as hard as I could. A moment later I was hopping round on three legs howling with pain, for a hunch of the quills had gone right into my paw, where they were still sticking, one coming out on the other side.

My father laughed, but my mother drew out the quills with her teeth, and that hurt worse than anything; and all day, whenever she found a particularly fat lily bulb, she gave it to me. For my part, I could only dig for the bulbs with my left paw, and it was ever so many days before I could run on all four feet again.

All these things must have happened when I was very young--less than three months old--because we were still living in the same place, whereas when summer came we moved away, as bears always do, and had no fixed home during the hot months.

Bear-cubs are born when the mother is still in her winter den, and they are usually five or six weeks old before they come out into the world at all. Even then at first, when the cubs are very young, the family stays close at home, and for some time I imagine that the longest journey I made was when I tumbled those fifty feet downhill. Father or mother might wander away alone in the early morning or evening for a while, but for the most part we were all four at home by the rock and the cedar-trees, with the bare brown tree-trunks growing up all round out of the bare brown mountain-sides, and Kahwa and I spending our time lying sleepily cuddled up to mother, or romping together and wishing we could catch squirrels.

There were a great many squirrels about--large gray ones mostly; but living in a fir-tree close by us was a black one with a deplorable temper.

Every day he used to come and quarrel with us. Whenever he had nothing particular to do, he would say to himself, "I'll go and tease those old bears." And he did. His plan was to get on our trees from behind, where we could not see him, then to come round on our side about five or six feet from the ground, just safely out of reach, and there, hanging head downwards, call us every name he could think of. Squirrels have an awful vocabulary, but I never knew one that could talk like Blacky. And every time he thought of something new to say he waved his tail at us in a way that was particularly aggravating. You have no idea how other animals poke fun at us because we have no tails, and how sensitive we really are on the subject. They say that it was to hide our lack of tail that we originally got into the habit of sitting up on our haunches whenever we meet a stranger.

Very soon we began to be taken out on long excursions, going all four together, as I have said, and then we began to learn how much that is nice to eat there is in the world.

You have probably no idea, for instance, how many good things there may be under one rotting log. Even if you do not get a mouse or a chipmunk, you are sure of a fringe of greenstuff which, from lack of sunlight, has grown white and juicy, and almost as sure of some mushrooms or other fungi, most of which are delicious. But before you can touch them you have to look after the insects. Mushrooms will wait, but the sooner you catch beetles, and earwigs, and ants, and grubs, the better. It is always worth while to roll a log over, if you can, no matter how much trouble it costs; and a big stone is sometimes nearly as good.

Insects, of course, are small, and it would take a lot of ants, or even beetles, to make a meal for a bear; but they are good, and they help out. Some wild animals, especially those which prey upon others, eat a lot at one time, and then starve till they can kill again. A bear, on the other hand, is wandering about for more than half of the twenty-four hours, except in the very heat of summer, and he is eating most of the while that he wanders. The greater part of his food, of course, is greenstuff--lily bulbs, white camas roots, wild-onions, and young shoots and leaves. As he walks he browses a mouthful of young leaves here, scratches up a root there, tears the bark off a decaying tree and eats the insects underneath, lifts a stone and finds a mouse or a lizard beneath, or loiters for twenty minutes over an ant-hill. With plenty of time, he is never in a hurry, and every little counts.

But most of all in summer I used to love to go down to the stream. In warm weather, during the heat of the day, bears stay in the shelter of thickets, among the brush by the water or under the shade of a fallen tree. As the sun sank we would move down to the stream, and lie all through the long evening in the shallows, where the cold water rippled against one's sides. And along the water there was always something good to eat--not merely the herbage and the roots of the water-plants, but frogs and insects of all sorts among the grass. Our favorite bathing-place was just above a wide pool made by a beaver-dam. The pool itself was deep in places, but before the river came to it, it flowed for a hundred yards and more over a level gravel bottom, so shallow that even as a cub I could walk from shore to shore without the water being above my shoulders. At the edge of the pool the same black and white kingfisher was always sitting on the same branch when we came down, and he disliked our coming, and chirred at us to go away. I used to love to pretend not to understand him, and to walk solemnly through the water underneath and all round his branch. It made him furious, and sent him chirring upstream to find another place to fish, where there were no idiotic bear-cubs who did not know any better than to walk about among his fish.

Here, too, my father and mother taught us to fish; but it was a long time before I managed to catch a trout for myself. It takes such a dreadful lot of sitting still. Having found where a fish is lying, probably under an overhanging branch or beneath the grass jutting out from the bank, you lie down silently as close to the edge of the water as you can get, and slip one paw in, ever so gradually, behind the fish, and move it towards him gently--gently. If he takes fright and darts away, you leave your paw where it is, or move it as close to the spot where he was lying as you can reach, and wait. Sooner or later he will come back, swimming downstream and then swinging round to take his station almost exactly in the same spot as before. If you leave your paw absolutely still, he does not mind it, and may even, on his return, come and lie right up against it. If so, you strike at once. More probably he will stop a few inches or a foot away. If you have already reached as far as you can towards him, then is the time that you need all your patience. Again and again he darts out to take a fly from the surface of the water or swallow something that is floated down to him by the current, and each time that he comes back he may shift his position an inch or two. At last he comes to where you can actually crook your claws under his tail. Ever so cautiously you move your paw gently half way up towards his head, and then, when your claws are almost touching him, you strike-- strike, once and hard, with a hooking blow that sends him whirling like a bar of silver far out on the bank behind you. And trout is good- -the plump, dark, pink-banded trout of the mountain streams. But you must not strike one fraction of a second too soon, for if your paw has more than an inch to travel before the claws touch him he is gone, and all you feel is the flip of a tail upon the inner side of the paw, and all your time is wasted.

It is hard to learn to wait long enough, and I know that at first I used to strike at fish that were a foot away, with no more chance of catching them than of making supper off a waterfall. But father and mother used to catch a fish apiece for us almost every evening, and gradually Kahwa and I began to take them for ourselves.

Then, as the daylight faded, the beavers came out upon their dam and played about in the pool, swimming and diving and slapping the surface with their tails with a noise like that of an osprey when he strikes the water in diving for a fish. But though they had time for play, they were busy folk, the beavers. Some of them were constantly patching and tinkering at the dam, and some always at work, except when the sun was up, one relieving another, gnawing their way with little tiny bites steadily through one of the great trees that stood by the water's edge, and always gnawing it so that when, after weeks of labor, it fell, it never failed to fall across the stream precisely where they wanted it. If an enemy appeared--at the least sign or smell of wolf or puma--there would be a loud ringing slap from one of the tails upon the water, and in an instant every beaver had vanished under water and was safe inside the house among the logs of the dam, the door of which was down below the surface.

Us bears they were used to and did not mind; but they never let us come too near. Sitting safely on the top of their piled logs, or twenty feet away in the water, they would talk to us pleasantly enough; but-- well, my father told me that young, very young, beaver was good eating and I imagine that the beavers knew that we thought so, and were afraid, perhaps, that we might not be too particular about the age.

As the dusk changed to darkness we would leave the water and roam over the hillsides, sometimes sleeping through the middle hours of the night, but in summer more often roaming on, to come back to the stream for a while just before the sun was up, and then turning in to sleep till he went down again.

Those long rambles in the summer moonlight, or in the early dawn when everything reeked with dew, how good they were! And when the afternoon of a broiling day brought a thunderstorm, the delight of the smell of the moist earth and the almost overpowering scent of the pines! And when the berries were ripe--blueberries, cranberries, wild-raspberries, and, later in the year, elderberries--no fruit, nor anything else to eat, has ever tasted as they did then in that first summer when I was a cub.

CHAPTER III.

THE COMING OF MAN.

Summer was far advanced. We had had a week or two of hot, dry weather, during which we had wandered abroad, spending the heat of the days asleep in the shadow of cool brushwood down by the streams, and in the nights and early mornings roaming where we would. Ultimately we worked round to the neighborhood of our home, and went to see if all was right there, and to spend one day in the familiar place.

It was in the very middle of the day--a sultry day, when the sun was blazing hot--that we were awakened by the sound of somebody coming through the bushes. The wind was blowing towards us, so that long before he came in sight we knew that it was a bear like ourselves. But what was a bear doing abroad at high noon of such a day, and crashing through the bushes in that headlong fashion? Something extraordinary must have happened to him, and we soon learned that indeed something had.

Coming plunging downhill with the wind behind him, he was right on us before he knew we were there. He was one of our cousins--a cinnamon--and we saw at once that he was hurt, for he was going on three legs, holding his left fore-paw off the ground. It was covered with blood and hung limply, showing that the bone was broken. He was so nervous that at sight of us he threw himself up on his haunches and prepared to fight; but we all felt sorry for him, and he soon quieted down.

"Whatever has happened to you?" asked my father, while we others sat and listened.

"Man!" replied Cinnamon, with a growl that made my blood run cold.

Man! Father had told us of man, but he had never seen him; nor had his father or his grandfather before him. Man had never visited our part of the mountains, as far as we knew, but stories of him we had heard in plenty. They had been handed down in our family from generation to generation, from the days when our ancestors lived far away from our present abiding-place; and every year, too, the animals that left the mountains when the snow came brought us back stories of man in the spring. The coyotes knew him and feared him; the deer knew him and trembled at his very name; the pumas knew him and both feared and hated him. Everyone who knew him seemed to fear him, and we had caught the fear from them, and feared him, too, and had blessed ourselves that he did not come near us.

And now he was here! And poor Cinnamon's shattered leg was evidence that his evil reputation was not unjustified.

Then Cinnamon told us his story.

He had lived, like his father and grandfather before him, some miles away on the other side of the high range of mountains behind us; and there he had considered himself as safe from man as we on our side had supposed ourselves to be. But that spring when he awoke he found that during the winter the men had come. They were few in the beginning, he said, and he had first heard of them as being some miles away. But more came, and ever more; and as they came they pushed farther and farther into the mountains. What they were doing he did not know, but they kept for the most part along by the streams, where they dug holes everywhere. No, they did not live in the holes. They built themselves places to live in out of trees which they cut down and chopped into lengths and piled together. Why they did that, when it was so much easier to dig comfortable holes in the hillside, he did not know; but they did. And they did not cut down the trees with their teeth like beavers, but took sticks in their hands and beat them till they fell!

Yes, it was true about the fires they made. They made them every day and all the time, usually just outside the houses that they built of the chopped trees. The fires were terrible to look at, but the men did not seem to be afraid of them. They stood quite close to them, especially in the evenings, and burned their food in them before they ate it.

We had heard this before, but had not believed it. And it was true, after all! What was still more wonderful, Cinnamon said that he had gone down at night, when the men were all asleep in their chopped-tree houses, and, sniffing round, had found pieces of this burnt food lying about, and eaten them, and--they were very good! So good were they that, incredible as it might seem, Cinnamon had gone again and again, night after night, to look for scraps that had been left lying about.

On the previous night he had gone down as usual after the men, as he supposed, were all asleep, but he was arrested before he got to the houses themselves by a strong smell of the burnt food somewhere close by him. The men, he explained, had cut down the trees nearest to the stream to build their houses with, so that between the edge of the forest and the water there was an open space dotted with the stumps of the trees that had been felled, which stuck up as high as a bear's shoulder from the ground. It was just at the edge of this open space that he smelled the burnt food, and, sure enough, on one of the nearest stumps there was a bigger lump of it than any he had ever seen. Naturally, he went straight up to it.

Just as he got to it he heard a movement between him and the houses, and, looking round, he saw a man lying flat on the ground in such a way that he had hitherto been hidden by another stump. As Cinnamon looked he saw the man point something at him (yes, unquestionably, the dreadful thing we had heard of--the thunder-stick--with which man kills at long distances), and in a moment there was a flash of flame and a noise like a big tree breaking in the wind, and something hit his leg and smashed it, as we could see. It hurt horribly, and Cinnamon turned at once and plunged into the wood. As he did so there was a second flash and roar, and something hit a tree-trunk within a foot of his head, and sent splinters flying in every direction.

Since then Cinnamon had been trying only to get away. His foot hurt him so that he had been obliged to lie down for a few hours in the bushes during the morning; but now he was pushing on again, only anxious to go somewhere as far away from man as possible.

While he was talking, my mother had been licking his wounded foot, while father sat up on his haunches, with his nose buried in the fur of his chest, grumbling and growling to himself, as his way was when he was very much annoyed. I have the same trick, which I suppose I inherited from him. We cubs sat shivering and whimpering, and listening terror-stricken to the awful story.

What was to be done now? That was the question. How far away, we asked, were the men? Well, it was about midnight when Cinnamon was wounded, and now it was noon. Except the three or four hours that he had lain in the bushes, he had been travelling in a straight line all the time, as fast as he could with his broken leg. And did men travel fast? No; they moved very slowly, and always on their hind-legs. Cinnamon had never seen one go on all fours, though that seemed to him as ridiculous as their building houses of chopped trees instead of making holes in the ground. They very rarely went about at night, and Cinnamon did not believe any of them had followed him, so there was probably no immediate danger. Moreover, Cinnamon explained, they seldom moved far away from the streams, and they made a great deal of noise wherever they went, so that it was easy to hear them. Besides which, you could smell them a long way off. It did not matter if you had never smelled it before: any bear would know the man-smell by the first whiff he got of it.

All this was somewhat consoling. It made the danger a little more remote, and, especially, it reduced the chance of our being taken by surprise. Still, the situation was bad enough as it stood, for the news changed the whole color and current of our lives. Hitherto we had gone without fear where we would, careless of anything but our own inclinations. Now a sudden terror had arisen, that threw a shadow over every minute of the day and night. Man was near--man, who seemed love to kill, and who could kill; not by his strength, but by virtue of some cunning which we could neither combat nor understand. Thereafter, though perhaps man's name might not be mentioned between us from one day to another, I do not think there was a minute when we were not all more or less on the alert, with ears and nostrils open for an indication of his dreaded presence.

Though Cinnamon thought we could safely stay where we were, he proposed himself to push on, farther away from the neighborhood of the hated human beings. In any emergency he was sadly crippled by his broken leg, and--at least till that was healed--he preferred to be as remote from danger as possible.

After he was gone my father and mother held council. There was no more sleep for us that day, and in the evening, when we started out on our regular search for food, it was very cautiously, and with nerves all on the jump. It was a trying night. We went warily, with our heads ever turned up-wind, hardly daring to dig for a root lest the sound of our digging should fill our ears so that we would not hear man's approach; and when I stripped a bit of bark from a fallen log to look for beetles underneath, and it crackled noisily as it came away, my father growled angrily at me and mother cuffed me from behind.

I remember, though, that they shared the beetles between them.

I need not dwell on the days of anxiety that followed. I do not remember them much myself, except that they were very long and nerve-racking. I will tell you at once how it was that we first actually came in contact with man himself.

In the course of my life I have reached the conclusion that nearly all the troubles that come to animals are the result of one of two things--either of their greediness or their curiosity. It was curiosity which led me into the difficulty with Porcupine. It was Cinnamon's greediness that got his leg broken for him. Our first coming in contact with man was the result, I am afraid, of both--but chiefly of our curiosity.

During the days that followed our meeting with Cinnamon, while we were moving about so cautiously, we were also all the time (and, though we never mentioned the fact, we all knew that we were) gradually working nearer to the place where Cinnamon had told us that man was. I knew what was happening, but would not have mentioned it for worlds, lest if we talked about it we should change our direction. And I wanted--yes, in spite of his terrors--I wanted to see man just once. Also--I may as well confess it--there were memories of what Cinnamon had said of that wonderful burnt food.

Some ten or twelve days must have passed in this way, when one morning, after we had been abroad for three or four hours, and the sun was just getting up, we heard a noise such as we had never heard before. Chuck! chuck! chuck! It came at regular intervals for a while, then stopped and began again. What could it be? It was not the noise of a woodpecker, nor that which a beaver makes with its tail. Chuck! chuck! chuck! It was not the clucking of a grouse, though perhaps more like that than anything else, but different, somehow, in quality. Chuck! chuck! chuck! I think we all knew in our hearts that it had something to do with man.

The noise came from not far away, but the wind was blowing across us. So we made a circle till it blew from the noise to us; and suddenly in one whiff we all knew that it was man. I felt my skin crawling up my spine, and I saw my father's nose go down into his chest, while the hair on his neck and shoulders stood out as it only could do in moments of intense excitement.

Slowly, very slowly, we moved towards the noise, until at last we were so close that the smell grew almost overpowering. But still we could not see him, because of the brushwood. Then we came to a fallen log and, carefully and silently we stepped on to it--my father and mother first, then I, then Kahwa. Now, by standing up on our hind-feet, our heads--even mine and Kahwa's--were clear of the bushes, and there, not fifty yards away from us, was man. He was chopping down a tree, and that was the noise that we had heard. He did not see us, being too intent on his work. Chuck! chuck! chuck! He was striking steadily at the tree with what I now know was an axe, but which at the time we all supposed to be a thunder-stick, and at each blow the splinters of wood flew just as Cinnamon had told us. After a while he stopped, and stooped to pick something off the ground. This hid him from my sight, and from Kahwa's also, so she strained up on her tiptoes to get another look at him. In doing so her feet slipped on the bark of the log, and down she came with a crash that could have been heard at twice his distance from us, even if the shock had not knocked a "Wooff!" out of her as she fell. The man instantly stood up and turned round, and, of course, found himself staring straight into our faces.

He did not hesitate a moment, but dropped his axe and ran. I think he ran as fast as he could, but what Cinnamon said was true: he went, of course, on his hind-legs, and did not travel fast. It was downhill, and running on your hind-legs for any distance downhill is an awkward performance at best.

We, of course, followed our impulse, and went after him. We did not want him in the least. We would not have known what to do with him if we had him. But you know how impossible it is to resist chasing anything that runs away from you. We could easily have caught him had we wished to, but why should we? Besides, he might still have another thunder-stick concealed about him. So we just ran fast enough to keep him running. And as we ran, crashing through the bushes, galloping down hill, with his head rising and falling as he leaped along ahead of us, the absurdity of it got hold of me, and I yelped with excitement and delight. To be chasing man, of all things living--man--like this! And I could hear my father "wooffing" to himself at each gallop with amusement and satisfaction.

Very soon, however, we smelled more men. Then we slowed down, and presently there came in sight what we knew must be one of the chopped-tree houses. So we stood and watched, while the man, still running as if we were at his very heels, tore up to the house, and out from behind it came three or four others. We could see them brandishing their arms and talking very excitedly. Then two of them plunged into the house, and came out with--yes, there could be no doubt of it; these were the real things--the dreaded thunder-sticks themselves.

Then we knew that it was our turn to run; and we ran.

Back up the hill we went, much faster than we had come down; for we were running for our own lives now, and bears like running uphill best. On and on we went, as fast as we could go. We had no idea at how long a distance man could hit us with the thunder-sticks, but we preferred to be on the safe side, and it must have been at least two hours before we stopped for a moment to take breath. And when a bear is in a hurry, two hours, even for a cub, mean more than twenty miles.

CHAPTER IV.

THE FOREST FIRE.

Though we had come off so happily from our first encounter with man, none the less we had no desire to see him again. On the contrary, we determined to keep as far away from him as possible. For my part, I confess that thoughts of him were always with me, and every thought made the skin crawl up my back.

Nor was I the only one of the family who was nervous. Father and mother had
become so changed that they were gruff and bad-tempered; and all the pleasure and light-heartedness seemed to have gone out of our long rambles. There was no more romping and rolling together down the hillsides. If Kahwa and I grew noisy in our play, we were certain to be stopped with a "Wooff, children! be quiet." The fear of man was always with us, and his presence seemed to pervade the whole of the mountains.

Soon, however, a thing happened which for a time at least drove man and everything else out of our minds.

We still lingered around the neighborhood of our home, because, I think, we felt safer there, where we knew every inch of the hills and every bush, and tree, and stone. It had been very hot for weeks, so that the earth was parched dry, and the streams had shrunk till, in places where torrents were pouring but a few weeks ago, there was now no more than a dribble of water going over the stones. During the day we hardly went about at all, but from soon after sunrise to an hour or so before sunset we kept in the shadow of the brushwood along the water's edge.

One evening the sun did not seem to be able to finish setting, but after it had gone down the red glow still stayed in the sky to westward, and instead of fading it glowed visibly brighter as the night went on. All night my father was uneasy, growling and grumbling to himself and continually sniffing the air to westward; but the atmosphere was stagnant and hot and dead all night, with not a breath of wind moving. When daylight came the glow died out of the western sky, but in place of it a heavy gray cloud hung over the farther mountains and hid their tops from sight. We went to bed that morning feeling very uncomfortable and restless, and by mid-day we were up again. And now we knew what the matter was.

A breeze had sprung up from the west, and when I woke after a few hours' sleep--sleep which had been one long nightmare of man and thunder-sticks and broken leg--the air was full of a new smell, very sharp and pungent; and not only was there the smell, but with the breeze the cloud from the west had been rolling towards us, and the whole mountain-side was covered with a thin haze, like a mist, only different from any mist that I had seen. And it was this haze that smelled so strongly. Instead of clearing away, as mist ought to do when the sun grows hot, this one became denser as the day went on, half veiling the sun itself. And we soon found that things--unusual things--were going on in the mountains. The birds were flying excitedly about, and the squirrels chattering, and everything was travelling from west to east, and on all sides we heard the same thing.

"The world's on fire! quick, quick, quick!" screamed the squirrels as they raced along the ground or jumped from tree to tree overhead. "Fire! fire!" called the myrtle-robin as it passed. "Firrrrrre!" shouted the blue jay. A coyote came limping by, yelping that the end of the world was at hand. Pumas passed snarling and growling angrily, first at us, and then over their shoulders at the smoke that rolled behind. Deer plunged up to us, stood for a minute quivering with terror, and plunged on again into the brush. Overhead and along the ground was an almost constant stream of birds and animals, all hurrying in the same direction.

Presently there came along another family of bears, the parents and two cubs just about the size of Kahwa and myself, the cubs whimpering and whining as they ran. The father bear asked my father if we were not going, too; but my father thought not. He was older and bigger than the other bear, and had seen a forest fire when he was a cub, and his father then had saved them by taking to the water.

"If a strong winds gets up," he said, "you cannot escape by running away from the fire, because it will travel faster than you. It may drive you before it for days, until you are worn out, and there's no knowing where it will drive you. It may drive you unexpectedly straight into man. I shall try the water."

The others listened to what he had to say, but they were too frightened to pay much attention, and soon went on again, leaving us to face the fire. And I confess that I wished that father would let us go, too.

Meanwhile the smoke had been growing thicker and thicker. It made eyes and throat smart, and poor little Kahwa was crying with discomfort and terror. Before sunset the air was so thick that we could not see a hundred yards in any direction, and as the twilight deepened the whole western half of the sky, from north to south and almost overhead, seemed to be aflame. Now, too, we could hear the roaring of the fire in the distance, like the noise the wind makes in the pine-trees before a thunderstorm. Then my father began to move, not away from the fire, however, but down the stream, and the stream ran almost due west straight towards it. What a terrible trip that was! The fire was, of course, much farther away than it looked; the smoke had been carried with the wind many miles ahead of the fire itself, and we could not yet see the flames, but only the awful glare in the sky. But, in my inexperience, I thought it was close upon us, and, with the dreadful roaring growing louder and louder in my ears, every minute was an agony.

[Illustration: "NOT FIFTY YARDS AWAY WAS MAN."]

But my father and mother went steadily on, and there was nothing to do but to follow them. Sometimes we left the stream for a little to make a short-cut, but we soon came back to it, and for the most part we kept in the middle of the water, or where it was deep close to the bank.

At last we reached our pool above the beaver-dam, and here, feeling his way cautiously well out into the middle, till he found a place where it was just deep enough for Kahwa and me to be able to lift our heads above the water, father stopped. By this time the air was so hot that it was hard to breathe without dipping one's mouth constantly in the water, and for the roaring of the flames I could not hear Kahwa whimpering at my side, or the rush of the stream below the dam. And we soon found that we were not alone in the pool. My friend the kingfisher was not there, but close beside us were old Grey Wolf and his wife, and, as I remembered that Grey Wolf was considered the wisest animal in the mountains, I began to feel more comfortable, and was glad that we had not run away with the others. The beavers--what a lot of them there were!--were in a state of great excitement, climbing out on to the top of the dam and slapping the logs and the water with their tails, then plunging into the water, only to climb out again and plunge in once more. Once a small herd of deer, seven or eight of them, came rushing into the water, evidently intending to stay there, but their courage failed them. Whether it was the proximity of Grey Wolf or whether it was mere nervousness I do not know, but after they had settled down in the water one of them was suddenly panic-stricken, and plunged for the bank and off into the woods, followed by all the rest.

When we reached the pool there was still one ridge or spur of the mountains between us and the fire, making a black wall in front of us, above which was nothing but a furnace of swirling smoke and red-hot air. It seemed as if we waited a long time for the flames to top that wall, because, I suppose, they travelled slowly down in the valley beyond, where they did not get the full force of the wind. Then we saw the sky just above the top of the wall glowing brighter from red to yellow; then came a few scattered, tossing bits of flame against the glow and the swirling smoke; and then, with one roar, it was upon us. In an instant the whole line of the mountain ridge was a mass of flame, the noise redoubled till it was almost deafening, and, as the wind now caught it, the fire leaped from tree to tree, not pausing at one before it swallowed the next, but in one steady rush, without check or interruption, it swept over the hill-top and down the nearer slope, and instantaneously, as it seemed, we were in the middle of it.

I remember recalling then what my father had said to the other bears about not being able to run away from the fire if the wind were blowing strongly.

Had we not been out in the middle of the pool, we must have perished. The fire was on both sides of the stream--indeed, as we learned later, it reached for many miles on both sides, and where there was only the usual width of water the flames joined hand across it and swept up the stream in one solid wall. Where we were was the whole width of the pool, while, besides, the beavers had cut down the larger trees immediately near the water, so there was less for the fire to feed upon. But even so I did not believe that we could come through alive. It was impossible to open my eyes above water, and the hot air scorched my throat. There was nothing for it but to keep my head under water and hold my breath as long as I could, then put my nose out just enough to breathe once, and plunge it in again. How long that went on I do not know, but it seemed to me ages; though the worst of it can only have lasted for minutes. But at the end of those minutes all the water in that huge pool was hot.

I saw my father raising his head and shoulders slowly out of the water and beginning to look about him. That gave me courage, and I did the same. The first thing that I realized was that the roaring was less loud, and then, though it was still almost intolerably hot, I found that it was possible to keep one's head in the open air and one's eyes open. Looking back, I saw that the line of flame had already swept far away, and was even now surmounting the top of the next high ridge; and it was, I knew, at that moment devouring the familiar cedars by our home, just as it had devoured the trees on either side of the beavers' pool. On all sides of us the bigger trees were still in flames, and from everywhere thick white smoke was rising, and over all the mountain-side, right down to the water's edge, there was not one green leaf or twig. Everything was black. The brushwood was completely gone. The trees were no more than bare trunks, some of them still partially wreathed in flames. The whole earth was black, and from every side rose columns and jets and streams of smoke. It seemed incredible that such a change could have been wrought so instantaneously. It was awful. Just a few minutes and what had been a mountain-side clothed in splendid trees, making one dense shield of green, sloping down to the bottom-land by the stream, with its thickets of undergrowth, and all the long cool green herbage by the water, had been swept away, and in its place was only a black and smoking wilderness. And what we saw before our eyes was the same for miles and miles to north and south of us, for a hundred miles to the west from which the fire had come; and every few minutes, as long as the wind held, carried desolation another mile to eastward.

And what of all the living things that had died? Had the animals and birds that had passed us earlier in the day escaped? The deer which had fled from the pool at the last moment--they, I knew, must have been overtaken in that first terrible rush of the flames; and I wondered what the chances were that the bears who had declined to stay with us, the squirrels, the coyote, the pumas, and the hosts of birds that had been hurrying eastward all day, would be able to keep moving long enough to save themselves. And what of all the insects and smaller things that must be perishing by millions every minute? I do not know whether I was more frightened at the thought of what we had escaped or grateful to my father for the course he had taken.

It is improbable that I thought of all this at the time, but I know I was dreadfully frightened; and it makes me laugh now to think what a long time it was before we could persuade Kahwa to put her head above water and look about her. Our eyes and throats were horribly sore, but otherwise none of us was hurt. But though we were alive, life did not look very bright for us. Where should we go? That was the first question. And what should we find to eat in all this smoking wilderness? While we sat in the middle of the pool wondering what we could do or whether it would be safe to do anything, we saw Grey Wolf start to go away. He climbed out on the bank while his wife sat in the water and watched him. He got out safely, and then put his nose down to snuff at the ground. The instant his nose touched the earth he gave a yelp, and plunged back into the water again. He had burnt the tip of his nose, for the ground was baking hot, as we soon discovered for ourselves. When we first stepped out on shore, our feet were so wet that we did not feel the heat, but in a few seconds they began to dry, and then the sooner we scrambled back into the water again, the better.

How long it would have taken the earth to cool again I do not know. It was covered with a layer of burned stuff, ashes, and charred wood, which everywhere continued smouldering underneath, and all through the morning of the next day little spirals of smoke were rising from the ground in every direction. Fortunately, at mid-day came a thunderstorm which lasted well on towards evening, and when the rain stopped the ground had ceased smoking. Many of the trees still smouldered and burned inside. Sometimes the flame would eat its way out again to the surface, so that the tree would go on burning in the middle of the wet forest until it was consumed; and for days afterwards, on scratching away the stuff on the surface, we would come to a layer of half burned sticks that was still too hot to touch.

We of course kept to the stream. There along the edges we found food, for the rushes and grass and plants of all kinds had burned to the water-line, but below that the stems and roots remained fresh and good. But it was impossible to avoid getting the black dust into one's nose and mouth, and our throats and nostrils were still full of the smell of the smoke. No amount of water would wash it out. The effect of the thunderstorm soon passed off, and by the next day everything was as dry as ever, and the least puff of wind filled the air with clouds of black powder which made us sneeze, and, getting into our eyes, kept them red and sore. I do not think that in all my life I have spent such a miserable time as during those days while we were trying to escape from the region of the fire.

Of course, we did not know that there was any escape. Perhaps the whole world had burned. But my father was sure that we should get out of it some time or other if we only kept straight on. And keep on we did, hardly ever leaving the water, but travelling on and on up the stream as it got smaller and smaller, until finally there was no stream at all, but only a spring bubbling out of the mountain-side. So we crossed over the burnt ground until we came to the beginning of another stream on the other side, and followed that down just as we had followed the first one up. And perhaps the most dreadful thing all the time was the utter silence of the woods. As a rule, both day and night, they were full of the noises of other animals and birds, but now there was not a sound in all the mountains. We seemed to be the only living things left.

The stream which we now followed was that on which the men whom we had seen were camping, and presently we came to the place where they had been. The chopped-log house was a pile of ashes and half-burnt wood. About the ruins we found all sorts of curious things that were new to us--among them, things which I now know were kettles and frying-pans; and we came across lumps of their food, but it was all too much covered with the black powder to be eatable. There we stayed for the best part of a day, and then we went on without having seen a sign of man himself, and wondering what had become of him.

Seven or eight days had passed since the fire, when, the day after we passed the place where man had lived, we came to a beaver-dam across the stream, and the beavers told us that, some hours before the fire reached there, they had seen the men hurrying downstream, but they did not know whether they had succeeded in escaping or not. And now other life began to reappear. We met badgers and woodchucks and rats which had taken refuge in their holes, and had at first been unable to force their way out again through the mass of burnt stuff which covered the ground and choked up their burrows. The air, too, began to be full of insects, which had been safe underground or in the hearts of trees, and were now hatching out. And then we met birds--woodpeckers first, and afterwards jays, which were working back into the burnt district, and from them it was that we first learned for certain that it was only a burnt district, and that there was part of the world which had escaped. So we pushed on, until one morning, when daylight came, we saw in the distance a hill-top on which the trees still stood with all their leaves unconsumed. And how good and cool it looked!

We did not stop to sleep, but travelled on all through the day, going as fast as we could along the rocky edges of the stream, which was now almost wide enough to be a river, when suddenly we heard strange noises ahead of us, and we knew what the noises were, and that they meant man again. Men were coming towards us along the bank of the stream, so we had to leave it and hurry into the woods. There, though there was no shelter but the burnt tree-stumps, we were safe and all we had to do was to squat perfectly still, and it was impossible even for us, at a little distance, to distinguish each other from burnt tree-stumps. So we sat and watched the men pass. There were five of them, each carrying a bundle nearly as big as himself on his back, and they laughed and talked noisily as they passed, without a suspicion that four bears were looking at them from less than a hundred yards away.

As soon as they had passed, we went on again, and before evening we came to places where the trees were only partly burned; here and there one had escaped altogether. Then, close by the stream, a patch of willows was as green and fresh as if there had been no fire; and at last we had left the burnt country behind us. How good it was--the smell of the dry pine-needles and the good, soft brown earth underneath, and the delight of the taste of food that was once more free from smoke, and the glory of that first roll in the green grass among the fresh, juicy undergrowth by the water!

That next day we slept--really slept--for the first time since the night in the beavers' pool.

# CHAPTER V.

## KAHWA.

We soon found that the country which we were now in was simply full of animals. Of course it had had its share of inhabitants before the fire, and, in addition, all those that fled before the flames had crowded into it; besides which the beasts of prey from all directions were drawn towards the same place by the abundance of food which was easy to get. We heard terrible stories of sufferings and narrow escapes, and the poor deer especially, when they had at last won to a place of safety from the flames, were generally so tired and so bewildered that they fell an easy prey to the pumas and wolves. All night long the forest was full of the yelping of the coyotes revelling over the bodies of animals that the larger beasts had killed and only partly eaten, and every creature seemed to be quarrelling with those of its kind, the former inhabitants of the neighborhood resenting the intrusion of the newcomers. For ourselves, nobody attacked us. We found two other families of bears quite close to us, but though we did not make friends at first, they did not quarrel with us. We were glad enough to live in peace, and to be able to devote ourselves to learning something about the new country.

In general it was very much like the place that we had left--the same succession of mountain after mountain, all densely covered with trees, and with the streams winding down through gulch and valley. The stream that we had followed was now a river, broader all along its course than the beavers' pool which had saved our lives, and at one place, about two miles beyond the end of the burned region, it passed through a valley, wider than any that I had seen, with an expanse of level land on either side. Here it was, on this level bottom-land, that I first tasted what are, I think, next to honey, of all wild things the greatest treat that a bear knows--ripe blueberries. But this "berry-path," as we called it, was to play a very important part in my life, and I must explain.

We had soon learned that we were now almost in the middle of men. There was the party which had passed us going up the stream into the burned country. There were two more log-houses about a mile from the edge of the burned country, and therefore also behind us. There were others farther down the stream, and almost every day men passed either up or down the river, going from one set of houses to another. Finally we heard, and, before we had been there a week, saw with our own eyes, that only some ten miles farther on, where our stream joined another and made a mighty river, there was a town, which had all sprung up since last winter, in which hundreds of men lived together. This was the great draw-back to our new home. But if we went farther on, the chances were that we should only come to more and more men; and for the present, by lying up most of the day, and only going out at night in the direction of their houses, there was no difficulty in keeping away from them.

Familiarity with them indeed had lessened our terror. We certainly had no desire to hurt them, and they, as they passed up and down or went about their work digging in the ground along the side of the river or chopping down trees, appeared to give no thought to us; and with that fear removed, even though we kept constantly on the alert, lest they should unexpectedly come too near us, our life was happy and free from care. Father and mother grew to be like their old selves again, less gruff and nervous than they had been since the memorable day when we saw Cinnamon with his broken leg; and as for Kahwa and me, though we romped less than we used to do--for we were seven months old now, and at seven months a bear is getting to be a big and serious animal--we were as happy as two young bears could be. After a long hot day, during which we had been sleeping in the shade, what could be more delightful than to go and lie in the cool stream, where it flowed only a foot or so deep, and as clear as the air itself, over a firm sandy bottom? There were frogs, and snails, and beetles of all sorts, along the water's edge, and the juicy stems of the reeds and water-plants. Then, in the night we wandered abroad finding lily roots, and the sweet ferns, and camas, and mushrooms, with another visit to the river in the early morning and perhaps a trout to wind up with before the sun drove us under cover again. And above all there was the berry-patch.

The mere smell of a berry-patch at the end of summer, when the sun has been beating down all day, so that the air is heavy with the scent of the cooking fruit, is delicious enough, but it is nothing to the sweetness of the berries themselves.

It was in the evening, after our dip in the river, when twilight was shading into night, that we used to visit the patch. It was a great open space in a bend of the river, half a mile long and nearly as wide, without a tree on it, and nothing but just the blueberry bushes growing close together all over it, reaching about up to one's chest as one walked through, and every bush loaded with berries. Not only we, but every bear in the neighborhood, used to go there each evening--the two other families of whom I have spoken, and also two other single he-bears who had no families. One of these was the only animal in the neighborhood--except the porcupines, which every bear hates--whom I disliked and feared. He was a bad-tempered beast, bigger than father, with whom at our first meeting he wanted to pick a quarrel, while making friends with mother. She, however, would not have anything to say to him. When he was getting ready to fight my father--walking sideways at him and snarling, while my father, I am bound to confess, backed away--mother did not say a word, but went straight at him as she had rushed at the puma that day when she saved my life. Then father jumped at him also, and between them they bundled him along till he fairly took to his heels and ran. But whenever we met him after that--and we saw him every evening at the patch--he snarled viciously at us, and I, at least, was careful to keep father and mother between him and me. If he had caught any one of us alone, I believe he would have killed us; so we took care that he never should.

I can see the berry-patch now, lying white and shining in the moonlight, with here and there round the edges, and even sometimes pretty well out into the middle, if the night was not too light, the black spots showing where the bears were feeding. We enjoyed our feasts in silence, and beyond an occasional snapping of a twig, or the cry of some animal from the forest, or the screech of a passing owl, there was not a sound but that of our own eating. One night, however, there came an interruption.

It was bright moonlight, and we were revelling in our enjoyment of the fruit, but father was curiously restless. The air was very still, but in a little gust of wind early in the evening father declared that he had smelled man. As an hour passed and there was no further sign of him, however, we forgot him in the delight of the ripe berries. Suddenly from the other side of the patch, nearly half a mile away from us, rang out the awful voice of the thunder-stick. We did not wait to see what was happening, but made at all speed for the shelter of the trees, and tore on up the mountain slope. There was no further sound, but we did not dare to go back to the patch that night, nor did we see any of the other bears; so that it was not until some days afterwards that we heard that the thunder-stick had very nearly killed the mother of one of the other families. It had cut a deep wound in her neck, and she had saved herself only by plunging into the woods. If we had known all this at the time, I doubt if we should have gone back to the berry-patch as we did on the very next night.

On our way to the patch we met the bad-tempered bear coming away from it. That was curious, and if it had been anybody else we should undoubtedly have asked him why he was leaving the feast at that time in the evening. Had we done so, it might have saved a lot of trouble. As it was, we only snarled back at him as he passed snarling by us, and went on our way. We were very careful, however, and took a long time to make our way out of the trees down to the edge of the bushes; but there was no sound to make us uneasy, nor any smell of man in such wind as blew. Of course we took care to approach the patch at the farthest point from where we had heard the thunder-stick on the night before. It was a cloudy night, and the moon shone only at intervals. Taking advantage of a passing cloud, we slipped out from the cover of the trees into the berry-bushes. We could see no other bears, but they might be hidden by the clouds. In a minute, however, the moon shone out, and had there been any others there--at least, as far out from the edge as ourselves--we must have been able to see them. Certainly, alas! we were seen, for even as I was looking round the patch in the first ray of the moonlight to see if any of our friends were there, the thunder-stick rang out again, and once more we plunged for the trees. But this time the sound was much nearer, and there was a second report before we were well into the shadow, and then a third. So terrified were we that there was no thought of stopping, but after we got into the woods we kept straight on as fast as we could go, father and mother in front, I next, and Kahwa behind; and none of us looked back, for we heard the shouts of men and the crashing of branches as they ran, and again and again the thunder-stick spoke.

Suddenly I became aware that Kahwa was not behind me. I stopped and looked round, but she was nowhere to be seen. I remembered having heard her give a sudden squeal, as if she had trodden on something sharp, but I had paid no attention to it at the time. Now I became frightened, and called to father and mother to stop. They were a long way ahead, and it was some time before I could get near enough to attract their attention and tell them that Kahwa was missing.

Mother wished to charge straight down the hill again at the men, thunder-sticks or no thunder-sticks; but father dissuaded her, and at last we began to retrace our steps cautiously, keeping our ears and noses open for any sign either of Kahwa or of man. As we came near the edge of the wood, noises reached us--shouts and stamping; and then, mixed with the other sounds, I clearly heard Kahwa's voice. She was crying in anger and pain, as if she was fighting, and fighting desperately. A minute later we were near enough to see, and a miserable sight it was that we saw.

Out in the middle of the berry-patch, in the brilliant moonlight, was poor Kahwa with four men. They had fastened ropes around her, and two of them at the end of one rope on one side, and two at the end of one on the other, were dragging her across the middle of the patch. She was fighting every inch of the way, but her struggles against four men were useless, and slowly, yard by yard, she was being dragged away from us.

But if she could not fight four men, could not we? There were four of us, and I said so to my father. But he only grunted, and reminded me of the thunder-sticks. It was only too true. Without the thunder-sticks we should have had no difficulty in meeting them, but with those weapons in their hands it would only be sacrificing our lives in vain to attempt a rescue. So there we had to stand and watch, my mother all the time whimpering and my father growling, and sitting up on his haunches and rubbing his nose in his chest. We dared not show ourselves in the open, so we followed the edge of the patch, keeping alongside of the men, but in the shadow of the trees. They pulled Kahwa across the middle of the patch into the woods on the other side, and down to the riverbank, where, we knew, there began an open path which the men had beaten in going to and from their houses half a mile farther on. Here there were several houses in a bunch together. Inside one of these they shut her, and then all went in to another house themselves. We stayed around, and two or three times later on we saw one or more of the men come out and stand for a while at Kahwa's door listening; but at last they came out no more, and we saw the lights go out in their house, and we knew that the men had gone to sleep.

Then we crept down cautiously till we could hear Kahwa whimpering and growling through the walls. My mother spoke to her, and there was silence for a moment, and then, when mother spoke again, the poor little thing recognized her voice and squealed with delight. But what could we do? We talked to her for awhile, and tried to scratch away the earth from round the wall, in the hope of getting at her; but it was all useless, and as the day began to dawn nothing remained but to make off before the men arose, and to crawl away to hide ourselves in the woods again.

What a wretched night that was! Hitherto I do not think that I had thought much of Kahwa. I had taken her as a matter of course, played with her and quarrelled with her by turns, without stopping to think what life might be without her. But now I thought of it, and as I lay awake through the morning I realized how much she had been to me, and wondered what the men would do with her. Most of all I wondered why they should have wanted to catch her at all. We had no wish to do them any harm. We were nobody's enemy; least of all was little Kahwa. Why could not men live in peace with us as we were willing to live in peace with them?

Long before it was dusk next evening we were in the woods as near to the men's houses as we dared to go, but we could hear no sound of my sister's voice. There appeared to be only one man about the place, and he was at work chopping wood, until just at sunset, when the other three men came back from down the stream, and we noticed that they carried long ropes slung over their arms. Were those the ropes with which they had dragged Kahwa the night before? If so, had they again, while we slept, dragged her off somewhere else? We feared it must be so.

Impatiently we waited until it was dark enough to trust ourselves in the open near the houses, and then we soon knew that our fears were justified. The door of the house in which Kahwa had been shut was open; the men went in and out of it, and evidently Kahwa was not there. Nor was there any trace of her about the buildings. So under my father's guidance we started on the path down the stream by which the three men had returned, and it was not long before we found the marks of where she had struggled against her captors, and in places the scent of her trail was still perceptible, in spite of the strong man-smell which pervaded the beaten path.

So we followed the trail down until we came to more houses; then made a circuit and followed on again, still finding evidence that she had passed. Soon we came to more houses, at ever shortening intervals, until the bank of the stream on both sides was either continuously occupied by houses or showed traces of men being constantly at work there. And beyond was the town itself. It was of no use for us to go farther. In the town we could see lights streaming from many of the buildings, and the shouting of men's voices came to our ears. We wandered round the outskirts of the town till it was daylight, and then drew back into the hills and lay down again, very sad and hungry--for we had hardly thought of food--and very lonesome.

Kahwa, we felt sure, was somewhere among those houses in the town. But that was little comfort to us. And all the time we wondered what man wanted with her, and why he could not have left us to be happy, as we had been before he came.

CHAPTER VI.

LIFE IN CAMP.

One of the results of Kahwa's disappearance was to make me much more solitary than I had ever been before, not merely because I did not have her to play with, but now, for the first time, I took to wandering on excursions by myself. And these excursions all had one object:--to find Kahwa.

For some days after her capture we waited about the outskirts of the town nearly all night long; but on the third or fourth morning father made up his mind that it was useless, and, though mother persuaded him not to abandon the search for another night or two, he insisted after that on giving up and returning to the neighborhood where we had been living since the fire. So we turned our backs upon the town, and, for my part very reluctantly, went home.

The moon was not yet much past the full, and I can remember now how the berry-patch looked that night as we passed it, lying white and shining in the moonlight. We saw no other bears at it, and did not stop, but kept under the trees round the edges, and went on to our favorite resting-place, where, a few hundred yards from the river, a couple of huge trees had at some time been blown down. Round their great trunks as they lay on the ground, young trees and a mass of elder-bushes and other brushwood had sprung up, making a dense thicket. The two logs lay side by side, and in between them, with the tangle of bushes all round and the branches of the other trees overhead, there was a complete and impenetrable shelter.

We had used this place so much that a regular path was worn to it through the bushes. This night as we came near we saw recent prints of a bear's feet on the path, and the bear that made them was evidently a big one. From the way father growled when he saw them, I think he guessed at once whose feet they were. I know that I had my suspicions--suspicions which soon proved to be correct.

During our absence our enemy, the surly bear that I have spoken of, had taken it into his head that he would occupy our home. Of course he had lived in this district much longer than we, and, had this been his home when we first came, we should never have thought of disputing possession with him. But it had been our home now, so far as we had any regular home at this time of year, ever since our arrival after the fire, while he had lived half a mile away. Now, however, there he was, standing obstinately in the pathway, swinging his head from side to side, and evidently intending to fight rather than go away. We all stopped, my father in front, my mother next, and I behind. I have said that the stranger was bigger than my father, and in an ordinary meeting in the forest I do not think my father would have attempted to stand up to him; but this was different. It was our home, and we all felt that he had no right there, but that, on the contrary, he was behaving as he was out of pure bad temper and a desire to bully us and make himself unpleasant. Moreover, the events of the last few days had rendered my father and mother irritable, and they were in no mood to be polite to anybody.

Usually it takes a long time to make two bears fight. We begin slowly, growling and walking sideways towards each other, and only getting nearer inch by inch. But on this occasion there was not much room in the path, and father was thoroughly exasperated. He hardly waited at all, but just stood sniffing with his nose up for a minute to see if the other showed any sign of going away, and then, without further warning, threw himself at him. I had never seen my father in a real fight, and now he was simply splendid. Before the stranger had time to realize what was happening, he was flung back on his haunches, and in a moment they were rolling over and over in one mass in the bushes. At first it was impossible to see what was going on, but, in spite of the ferocity of my father's rush, it soon became evident that in the end the bigger bear must win. My father's face was buried in the other's left shoulder, and he had evidently got a good grip there; but he was almost on his back, for the stranger had worked himself uppermost, and we could see that he was trying to get his teeth round my father's fore-leg. Had he once got hold, nothing could have saved the leg, bone and all, from being crushed to pieces, and father, if not killed, would certainly have been beaten, and probably crippled for life. And sooner or later it seemed certain that the stranger would get his hold.

Then it was that my mother interfered. Hurling herself at him, she threw her whole weight into one swinging blow on the side of the big bear's head, and in another second had plunged her teeth into the back of his neck. My father's grip in the fleshy part of the shoulder, however painful it might be, had little real effect; but where my mother had attacked, behind the right ear, was a different matter. The stranger was obliged to leave my father's leg alone and to turn and defend himself against this new onslaught; but, big as he was, he now had more on his hands than he could manage. As soon as he turned his attention to my mother, my father let go of his shoulder, and in his turn tried to grip the other's fore-leg. There was nothing for the stranger to do now but to get out of it as fast as he could; and even I could not help admiring his strength as he lifted himself up and shook mother off as lightly as she would have shaken me. She escaped the wicked blow that he aimed at her, and dodged out of his reach, and my father, letting go his hold of the fore-leg, did the same. The stranger, with one on either side of him, backed himself against one of the fallen logs and waited for them to attack him. But that they had no wish to do. All that they wanted was that he should go away, and they told him so. They moved aside from the path on either hand to give him space to go, and slowly and surlily he began to move.

I was still standing in the pathway. Suddenly he made a movement as if to rush at me, but my father and mother jumped towards him simultaneously, while I plunged into the bushes, and he was compelled to turn and defend himself against my parents again. But they did not attack him, though they followed him slowly along the path. Every step or two he stopped to make an ugly start back at one or the other, but he knew that he was overmatched, and yard by yard he made off, my father and mother following him as far as the edge of the thicket, and standing to watch him out of sight. And I was glad when he was safely gone and they came back to me.

It was not a pleasant home-coming, and we were all restless and nervous for days afterwards; and then it was that I vowed to myself that, if I ever grew up and the opportunity came, I would wreak vengeance on that bear.

If we were all nervous, I was the worst, and in my restlessness took to going off by myself. Up to this time I do not think I had ever been a hundred yards away from one or other of my parents, and now, when I started out alone, it was always in horrible fear of meeting the big bear when there was no one to stand by me. Gradually, however, I acquired confidence in myself, making each night a longer trip alone, and each night going in the direction of the town. At last, one night, I found myself at the edge of the town itself, and now when I was alone I did not stop at the first building that I came to, but very cautiously--for the man-smell was thick around me, and terrified me in spite of myself--very cautiously I began to thread my way in between the buildings.[A] As I snuffed round each building, I found all sorts of new things to eat, with strange tastes, but most of them were good. That the men were not all asleep was plain from the shouts and noises which reached me at times from the centre of the big town, where, as I could see by occasional glimpses which I caught of the nearer buildings, many of the houses had bright lights streaming from them all night. Avoiding these, I wandered on, picking up things to eat, and all the while keeping ears and nose open for a sign of Kahwa.

[A] The new mining town or camp of the Far West has no long rows of houses or paved streets. The houses are built of logs or of boards, rarely more than one story high, and are set down irregularly. There maybe one more or less well-defined "street"--the main trail running through the camp--but even along that there will be wide gaps between the houses; while, for the rest, the buildings are at all sorts of angles, so that a man or a bear may wander through them as he pleases, regardless of whether he is following a "street" or not.

I stayed thus, moving in and out among the buildings, till dawn. Once a dog inside a house barked furiously as I came near, and I heard a man's voice speaking to it, and I hurried on. As the sky began to lighten, I made my way out into the woods again, and rejoined my father and mother before the sun was up. When I joined them, my father growled at me because I smelled of man.

The next night found me down in the town again. I began to know my way about. I learned which houses contained dogs, and avoided them. Other animals besides myself, I discovered, came into the town at night for the sake of the food which they found lying about-- coyotes and wood-rats, and polecats; but though bears would occasionally visit the buildings nearest to the woods, no other penetrated into the heart of the town as I did. It had a curious fascination for me, and gradually I grew so much at home, that even when a man came through the buildings towards me, I only slipped out of his way round a corner, and--for man's sight and smell are both miserably bad compared with ours--he never had a suspicion that I was near.

On the third or fourth night I had gone nearer to the lighted buildings than I had ever been before, when I heard a sound that made me stop dead and throw myself up on my haunches to listen. Yes, there could be no doubt of it! It was Kahwa's voice. Anyone who did not know her might have thought that she was angry, but I knew better. She was making exactly the noise that she used to make when romping with me, and I knew that she was not angry, but only pretending, and that she must be playing with someone. I suppose I ought to have been glad that she was alive and happy enough to be able to play, but it only enraged me and made me wonder who her playmates might be. Then gradually the truth, the incredible truth, dawned upon me. Truly incredible it seemed at first, but there could be no doubt of it. She was playing with man.

I could hear men's voices speaking to her as if in anger, and then I heard her voice and theirs in turn again, and at last I recognized that their anger was no more real than hers. The sounds came from where the lights were brightest, and it was long before I could make up my mind to go near enough to be able to see. At last, however, I crept to a place from which I could look out between two buildings, keeping in the deep shade myself, and I can see now every detail of what met my eyes as plainly as if it was all before me at this minute.

There was a building larger than those around it, with a big door wide open, and from the door and from the windows on either side poured streams of light out into the night. In the middle of the light, and almost in front of the door, was a group of five or six men, and in the centre of the group was Kahwa, tied to a post by a chain which was fastened to a collar round her neck. I saw a man stoop down and hold something out to her--presumably something to eat--and then, as she came to take it from the hand which he held out, he suddenly drew it away and hit her on the side of the head with his other hand. He did not hit hard enough to hurt her, and it was evidently done in play, because as he did it she got up on her hind-legs and slapped at him, first with one hand and then with the other, growling all the time in angry make-believe. Sometimes the man came too near, and Kahwa would hit him, and the other men all burst out laughing. Then I saw him walk deliberately right up to her, and they took hold of each other and wrestled, just as Kahwa and I used to do by the old place under the cedar-trees when we were little cubs. I could see, too, that now and then she was not doing her best, and did not want to hurt him, and he certainly did not hurt her.

At last the men went into the building, leaving Kahwa alone outside; but other men were continually coming out of, or going into, the open door, and I was afraid to approach her, or even to make any noise to tell her of my presence. So I sat in the shade of the buildings and watched. Nearly every man who passed stopped for a minute and spoke to her, but none except the man whom I had first seen tried to play with her or went within her reach. The whole thing seemed to me incredible, but there it was under my eyes, and, somehow, it made me feel terribly lonely--all the lonelier, I think, because she had these new friends; for as friends she undoubtedly regarded them, while I could not even go near enough to speak to her.

At last so many men came out of the building that I was afraid to stay. Some of them went one way, and some another, and I had to keep constantly moving my position to avoid being seen. In doing so I found myself farther and father away from the centre of the town, and nearer to the outskirts. The men shouted and laughed, and made so much noise that I did not dare to go back, but made my way out into the woods. And for the first time I did not go home to my father and mother, but stayed by myself in the brush.

The next evening I again made my way into the town, and once more saw the same sights as on the preceding night. This evening, however, there was a wind blowing, and it blew directly from me, as I stood in the same place, to Kahwa in front of the lighted door. Suddenly, while she was in the middle of her play, I saw her stop and begin to snuff up the wind with every sign of excitement. Then she called to me. Answer I dared not, but I knew that she had recognized me and would understand why I did not speak. While she was still calling to me, the man with whom she had been playing-- the same man as on the night before--came up and gave her a cuff on the head, and she lost her temper in earnest. She hit at him angrily, but he jumped out of her way (how I wished she had caught him!), and, after trying for awhile to tempt her with play again, he and the other men left her and went into the building. Then she gave all her time to me, and at last, when nobody was near, I spoke just loud enough for her to hear. She simply danced with excitement, running to the end of her chain toward me until it threw her back on to her hind-legs, circling round and round the stump to which she was fastened, and then charging out to the end of her chain again, all the time whimpering and calling to me in a way which made me long to go to her.

I did not dare to show myself, however, but waited until, as on the night before, just as it was beginning to get light, the men all came out of the building and scattered in different directions. This time, however, I did not go back to the woods, but merely shifted out of the men's way behind the dark corners of the buildings, hoping that somehow I would find an opportunity of getting to speak to Kahwa. At last the building was quiet, and only the man who had played with Kahwa seemed to be left, and I saw the lights inside begin to grow less. I hoped that then the door would be shut, and the man inside would go to sleep, as I knew that men did in other houses when the lights disappeared at night; but while there was still some light issuing from door and windows the man came out and went up to Kahwa, and, unfastening the chain from the stump, proceeded to lead her away somewhere to the rear of the building. She struggled and tried to pull away from him, but he jerked her along with the chain, and I could see that she was afraid of him, and did not dare to fight him in earnest, and bit by bit he dragged her along. I followed and saw him go to a sort of pen, or a small enclosure of high walls without any roof, in which he left her, and then went in to his own building. And soon I saw the last lights go out inside and everything was quiet.

I stole round to the pen and spoke to Kahwa through the walls. She was crazy at the sound of my voice, and could hear her running round and round inside, dragging the chain after her. Could she not climb out? I asked her. No; the walls were made of straight, smooth boards with nothing that she could get her claws into, and much too high to jump. But we found a crack close to the ground through which our noses would almost touch, and that was some consolation.

I stayed there as long as I dared, and told her all that had happened since she was taken away--of the fight with the strange bear, and how I had been in the town alone looking for her night after night; and she told me her story, parts of which I could not believe, though now I can understand them better.

What puzzled me, and at the time made me thoroughly angry, was the way in which she spoke of the man whom I had seen playing with her, and who had dragged her into the pen. She was afraid of him in a curious way--in much the same way as she was afraid of father or mother. The idea that she could feel any affection for him I would have scouted as preposterous; but after the experiences of the last few nights nothing seemed too wonderful to be true, and it was plain that all her thoughts centered in him and he represented everything in life to her. Without him she would have no food, but as it was she had plenty. He never came to her without bringing things to eat, delightful things sometimes; and in particular she told me of pieces of white stuff, square and rough like small stones, but sweeter and more delicious than honey. Of course, I know now that it was sugar; but as she told me about it then, and how good it was, and how the man always had pieces of it in his pockets, which he gave her while they were playing together, I found myself envying her, and even wishing that the man would take me to play with, too.

But as we talked the day was getting lighter, and promising to come again next night, I slipped away in the dawn into the woods.

Night after night I used to go and speak to Kahwa. Sometimes I did not go until it was nearly daylight, and she was already in her pen. Sometimes I went earlier, and watched her with the men before the door of the building, and often I saw the man who was her master playing with her and giving her lumps of sugar, and I could tell from the way in which she ate it how good it was. Many time I had narrow escapes of being seen, for I grew careless, and trotted among the houses as if I were in the middle of the forest. More than once I came close to a man unexpectedly, for the man-smell was so strong everywhere that a single man more or less in my neighborhood made no difference, and I had to trust to my eyes and ears entirely. Somehow, however, I managed always to keep out of their way, and during this time I used to eat very little wild food, living almost altogether on the things that I picked up in the town. And during all these days and nights I never saw my father or my mother.

Then one evening an eventful thing happened. The door of Kahwa's pen closed with a latch from the outside--a large piece of iron which lifted and fell, and was then kept in place by a block of wood. I had spent a great deal of time at that latch, lifting it with my nose, and biting and worrying it, in the hopes of breaking it off or opening the door; but when I did that I was always standing on my hind-legs, so as to reach up to it, with my fore-feet on the door, and, of course, my weight kept the door shut. But that never occurred to me. One evening, however, I happened to be standing up and sniffing at the latch, with my fore-feet not on the door itself, but on the wall beside the door. It happened that, just as I lifted the latch with my nose, Kahwa put her fore-feet against the door on the inside. To my astonishment, the door swung open into my face, and Kahwa came rolling out. If we had only thought it out, we could just as well have done that on the first night, instead of trying to reach each other for nearly two weeks through a narrow crack in the wall until nearly all the skin was rubbed off our noses.

However, it was done at last, and we were so glad that we thought of nothing else. Now we were free to go back into the woods and take up our old life again with father and mother. Would it not be glorious, I asked? Yes, she said, it would be glorious. To go off into the woods, and never, never, never, I said, see or think of man again.

Yes--yes, she said, but--Of course it would be very glorious, but--Well, there was the white stuff--the sugar--she could come back once in a while--just once in a while--couldn't she, to see the man and get a lump or two?

I am afraid I lost my temper. Here was what ought to have been a moment of complete happiness spoiled by her greediness. Of course she could not come back, I told her. If she did she would never get away a second time. We would go to father and mother and persuade them to move just as far away from man as they could. Instead of being delighted, the prospect only made her gloomy and thoughtful. Of course she wanted to see father and mother, but--but--but--There was always that "but"--and the thought of the man and the sugar.

While we were arguing, the time came when I usually left the town for the day, and the immediate thing to be done was to get away from that place and out into the woods, and all went well till we got to the last house in the town.

Now, however, Kahwa insisted on going up to snuff around this house. I warned her of the dog, but the truth was that she had grown accustomed to dogs, and I think had really lost her fear of men. So she went close up to the house, and began smelling round the walls to see if there was anything good to eat, while I stood back under the trees fretting and impatient of her delay.

Having sniffed all along one side of the house, she passed round the corner to the back. In turning the corner she came right upon the dog, who flew at her at once, though he was not much bigger than her head. Whether she was accustomed to dogs or not, the sudden attack startled her, and she turned round to run back to me. In doing so she just grazed the corner of the house, and the next instant she was rolling head over heels on the ground. The end of her chain had caught in the crack between the ends of two of the logs at the corner, and she was held as firmly as if she had been tied to her stump in front of the door. As she rolled over, the dog jumped upon her, small as he was, yelping all the time, and barking furiously. I thought it would only be a momentary delay, but the chain held fast, and all the while the dog's attacks made it impossible for her to give her attention to trying to tear it free.

A minute later, and the door of the house burst open, and a man came running out, carrying, to my horror, a thunder-stick in his hand. Kahwa and the dog were all mixed up together on the ground, and I saw the man stop and stand still a moment and point the thunder-stick at her. And then came that terrible noise of the thunder-stick speaking.

Too frightened to see what happened, I took to my heels, and plunged into the wood as fast as I could, without the man or the dog having seen me. I ran on for some distance till I felt safe enough to stop and listen, but there was not a sound, and no sign of Kahwa coming after me. I waited and waited until the sun came up, and still there was no sign of Kahwa, until at last I summoned up courage to steal slowly back again. As I came near I heard the dog barking at intervals, and then the voices of men. Very cautiously I crept near enough to get a view of the house from behind, and as I came in sight of the corner where Kahwa had fallen I saw her for the second time--just as on that wretched evening at the berry-patch-- surrounded by a group of three or four men. But this time they had no ropes round her, and were not trying to drag her away; only they stood talking and looking down at her, while she lay dead on the ground before them.

CHAPTER VII.

THE PARTING OF THE WAYS.

Now indeed I was truly lonely. During the three or four weeks that had passed since I had seen my father or mother, I had in a measure learned to rely upon myself; nor had I so far felt the separation keenly, because I knew that every evening I should see Kahwa. Now she was gone for ever. There was no longer any object in going into the town, and the terror of that last scene was still so vivid in my mind that I wished never to see man again.

It was true that I had feared man instinctively from the first, but familiarity with him had for a while overcome that fear. Now it returned, and with the fear was mingled another feeling--a feeling of definite hatred. Originally, though afraid of him, I had borne man no ill-will whatever, and would have been entirely content to go on living beside him in peace and friendliness, just as we lived with the deer and the beaver. Man himself made that impossible; and now I no longer wished it. I hated him--hated him thoroughly. Had it not been for dread of the thunder-sticks, I should have gone down into the town and attacked the first man that I met. I would have persuaded other bears to go with me to range through the buildings, destroying every man that we could find; and though this was impossible, I made up my mind that it would be a bad day for any man whom I might meet alone, when unprotected by the weapon that gave him so great an advantage.

Meanwhile my present business was, somehow and somewhere, to go on living. On that first evening, amid my conflict of emotions, it was some time before I could bring myself to turn my back definitely upon the town; for it was difficult to realize at once that there was in truth no longer any Kahwa there, nor any reason for my going again among the buildings, and it was late in the night before I finally started to look for my father and mother. I went, of course, to the place where I had left them, and where the fight with the stranger had taken place.

They were not there when I arrived, but I saw that they had spent the preceding day at home, and would, in all probability, be back soon after it was light. So I stayed in the immediate neighborhood, and before sunrise they returned. My mother was glad to see me, but I do not think I can say as much for my father. I told them where I had been, and of my visits to the town, and of poor Kahwa's death; and though at the time father did not seem to pay much attention to what I said, next day he suggested that we should move farther away from the neighborhood of men.

The following afternoon we started, making our way back along the stream by which we had descended, and soon finding ourselves once more in the region that had been swept by fire. It was still desolate, but the two months that had passed had made a wonderful difference. It was covered by the bright red flowers of a tall plant standing nearly as high as a bear's head, which shoots up all over the charred soil whenever a tract of forest is burned. Other undergrowth may come up in the following spring, but for the first year nothing appears except the red "fireweed," and that grows so thickly that the burnt wood is a blaze of color, out of which the blackened trunks of the old trees stand up naked and gaunt.

We passed several houses of men by the waterside, and gave them a wide berth. We learned from the beavers and the ospreys that a number of men had gone up the stream during the summer, and few had come back, so that now there must be many more of them in the district swept by the fire than there had been before. We did not wish to live in the burnt country, however, because there was little food to be found there, and under the fireweed the ground was still covered with a layer of the bitter black stuff, which, on being disturbed, got into one's throat and eyes and nostrils. So we turned southwards along the edge of the track of the fire, and soon found ourselves in a country that was entirely new to us, though differing little in general appearance from the other places with which we were familiar--the same unbroken succession of hills and gulches covered with the dense growth of good forest trees. It was, in fact, bears' country; and in it we felt at home.

For the most part we travelled in the morning and evening; but the summer was gone now, and on the higher mountains it was sometimes bitterly cold, so we often kept on moving all day. We were not going anywhere in particular: only endeavoring to get away from man, and, if possible, to find a region where he had never been. But it seemed as if man now was pushing in everywhere. We did not see him, but continually we came across the traces of him along the banks of the streams. The beavers, and the kingfishers, of course, know everything that goes on along the rivers. Nothing can pass upstream or down without going by the beaver-dams, and the beavers are always on the watch. You might linger about a beaver-dam all day, and except for the smell, which a man would not notice, you would not believe there was a beaver near. But they are watching you from the cracks and holes in their homes, and in the evening, if they are not afraid of you, you will be astonished to see twenty or thirty beavers come out to play about what you thought was an empty house. We never passed a dam without asking about man, and always it was the same tale. Men had been there a week ago, or the day before, or when the moon last was full. And the kingfishers and the ospreys told us the same things. So we kept on our way southward.

As the days went on I grew to think less of Kahwa; the memory of those nights spent in the town, with the lights, and the strange noises, and the warm man-smell all about me, began to fade until they all seemed more like incidents of a dream than scenes which I had actually lived through only a few weeks before. I began to feel more as I used to feel in the good old days before the fire, and came again to be a part of the wild, wholesome life of the woods. Moreover, I was growing; my mother said that I was growing fast. No puma would have dared to touch me now, and my unusual experiences about the town had bred in me a spirit of independence and self-reliance, so that other cubs of my own age whom we met, and who, of course, had lived always with their parents, always seemed to me younger than I; and certainly I was bigger and stronger than any first-year bear that I saw. On the whole, I would have been fairly contented with life had it not been for the estrangement which was somehow growing up between my father and myself. I could not help feeling that, though I knew not why, he would have been glad to have me go away again. So I kept out of his way as much as possible, seldom speaking to him, and, of course, not venturing to share any food that he found. On the first evening after my return he had rolled over an old log, and mother and I went up as a matter of course to see what was there; but he growled at me in a way that made me stand off while he and mother finished the fungi and the beetles. After that I kept my distance. It did not matter much, for I was well able to forage for myself. But I would have preferred to have him kinder. His unkindness, however, did not prevent him from taking for himself anything which he wanted that I had found. One day I came across some honey, from which he promptly drove me away, and I had to look on while he and mother shared the feast between them.

At last we came to a stream where the beavers told us that no man had been seen in the time of any member of their colony then living. The stream, which was here wide enough to be a river, came from the west, and for two or three days we followed it down eastwards, and found no trace or news of man; so we turned back up it again--

back past the place where we had first struck it--and on along its course for another day's journey into the mountains. It was, perhaps, too much to hope that we had lighted on a place where man would never come; but at least we knew that for a distance of a week's travelling in all directions he never yet had been, and it might be many years before he came. Meanwhile we should have a chance to live our lives in peace.

Here we stayed, moving about very little, and feeding as much as we could; for winter was coming on, and a bear likes to be fat and well fed before his long sleep. It rained a good deal now, as it always does in the mountains in the late autumn, and as a general rule the woods were full of mist all day, in which we went about tearing the roots out of the soft earth, eating the late blueberries where we could find them, and the cranberries and the elderberries, which were ripe on the bushes, now and then coming across a clump of nut-trees, and once in a while, the greatest of all treats, revelling in a feast of honey.

One morning, after a cold and stormy night, we saw that the tops of the highest mountains were covered with snow. It might be a week or two yet before the snow fell over the country as a whole, or it might be only a day or two; for the wind was blowing from the north, biting cold, and making us feel numb and drowsy. So my father decided that it was time to make our homes for the winter. He had already fixed upon a spot where a tree had fallen and torn out its roots, making a cave well shut in on two sides, and blocked on a third by another fallen log; and here, without thinking, I had taken it as a matter of course that we should somehow all make our winter homes together. But when that morning he started out, with mother after him, and I attempted to follow, he drove me away. I followed yet for a while, but he kept turning back and growling at me, and at last told me bluntly that I must go and shift for myself. I took it philosophically, I think, but it was with a heavy heart that I turned away to seek a winter home for myself.

It did not take me long to decide on the spot. At the head of a narrow gully, where at some time or other a stream must have run, there was a tree half fallen, and leaning against the hillside. A little digging behind the tree would make as snug and sheltered a den as I could want. So I set to work, and in the course of a few hours I had made a sufficiently large hollow, and into it I scraped all the leaves and pine-needles in the neighborhood, and, by working about inside and turning round and round, I piled them up on all sides until I had a nest where I was perfectly sheltered, with only an opening in front large enough to go in and out of. This opening I would almost close when the time came, but for the present I left it open and lived inside, sleeping much of the time, but still continuing for a week or ten days to go out in the mornings and evenings for food. But it was getting colder and colder, and the woods had become strangely silent. The deer had gone down to the lower ground at the first sign of coming winter, and the coyotes and the wolves had followed to spend the cold months in the foot-hills and on the plains about the haunts of man. The woodchucks were already asleep below-ground, and of the birds only the woodpeckers and the crossbills, and some smaller birds fluttering among the pine-branches, remained. There was a fringe of ice along the edges of the streams, and the kingfishers and the ospreys had both flown to where the waters would remain open throughout the year. The beavers had been very busy for some time, but now, if one went to the nearest dam in the evening, there was not a sign of life.

At last the winter came. It had been very cold and gray for a day or two, and I felt dull and torpid. And then, one morning towards mid-day, the white flakes began to fall. There had been a few little flurries of snow before, lasting only for a minute or two; but this was different. The great flakes fell slowly and softly, and soon the whole landscape began to grow white. Through the opening in my den I watched the snow falling for some time, but did not venture out; and as the afternoon wore on, and it only fell faster and faster, I saw that it would soon pile up and close the door upon me.

There was no danger of its coming in, for I had taken care that the roof overhung far enough to prevent anything falling in from above, and the den was too well sheltered for the wind to drift the snow inside. So I burrowed down into my leaves and pine-needles, and worked them up on both sides till only a narrow slit of an opening remained, and through this slit, sitting back on my haunches against the rear of the little cave I watched the white wall rising outside. All that night and all next day it snowed, and by the second evening there was hardly a ray of light coming in. I remember feeling a certain pride in being all alone, in the warm nest made by myself, for the first time in my life; and I sat back and mumbled at my paw, and grew gradually drowsier and drowsier, till I hardly knew when the morning came, for I was very sleepy and the daylight scarcely pierced the wall of snow outside. And before another night fell I was asleep, while outside the white covering which was to shut me in for the next four months at least, was growing thicker. Under it I was as safe and snug up there in the heart of the mountains as ever a man could be in any house that he might build.

CHAPTER VIII.

ALONE IN THE WORLD.

Have you any idea how frightfully stiff one is after nearly five months' consecutive sleep? Of course, a bear is not actually asleep for the greater part of the time, but in a deliciously drowsy condition that is halfway between sleeping and waking. It is very good. Of course, you lose all count and thought of time; days and weeks and months are all the same. You only know that, having been asleep, you are partly awake again. There is no light, but you can see the wall of your den in front of you, and dimly you know that, while all the world outside is snow-covered and swept with bitter winds, and the earth is gripped solid in the frost, you are very warm and comfortable. Changes of temperature do not reach you, and you sit and croon to yourself and mumble your paws, and all sorts of thoughts and tangled scraps of dreams go swimming through your head until, before you know it, you have forgotten everything and are asleep again.

Then again you find yourself awake. Is it hours or days or weeks since you were last awake? You do not know, and it does not matter. So you croon, and mumble, and dream, and sleep again; and wake, and croon, and mumble, and dream.

At last a day comes when you wake into something more like complete consciousness than you have known since you shut yourself up. There is a new feeling in the air; a sense of moisture and fresh smells are mingling with the warm dry scent of your den. And you are aware that you have not changed your position for more than a quarter of a year, but have been squatting on your heels, with your back against the wall and your nose folded into your paws across your breast; and you want to stretch your hind-legs dreadfully. But you do not do it. It is still too comfortable where you are. You may move a little, and have a vague idea that it might be rather nice outside. But you do not go to see; you only take the other paw into your mouth, and, still crooning to yourself, you are asleep again.

This happens again and again, and each time the change in the feeling of the air is more marked, and the scents of the new year outside grow stronger and more pungent. At last one day comes daylight, where the snow has melted from the opening in front of you, and with the daylight comes the notes of birds and the ringing of the woodpecker--rat-tat-tat-tat! rat-tat-tat-tat!--from a tree near by. But even these signs that the spring is at hand again would not tempt you out if it were not for another feeling that begins to assert itself, and will not let you rest. You find you are hungry, horribly hungry. It is of no use to say to yourself that you are perfectly snug and contented where you are, and that there is all the spring and summer to get up in. You are no longer contented. It is nearly five months since you had your last meal, and you will not have another till you go out for yourself and get it. Mumbling your paws will not satisfy you. There is really nothing for it but to get up.

But, oh, what a business it is, that getting up! Your shoulders are cramped and your back is stiff; and as for your legs underneath you, you wonder if they will really ever get supple and strong again. First you lift your head from your breast and try moving your neck about, and sniff at the walls of your den. Then you unfold your arms, and-- ooch!--how they crack, first one and then the other! At last you begin to roll from one side to the other, and try to stretch each hind-leg in turn; then cautiously letting yourself drop on all fours, you give a step, and before you know it you have staggered out into the open air.

It is very early in the morning, and the day is just breaking, and all the mountain-side is covered with a clinging pearly mist; but to your eyes the light seems very strong, and the smell of the new moist earth and the resinous scent of the pines almost hurt your nostrils. One side of the gully in front of you is brown and bare, but in the bottom, and clinging to the other side, are patches of moist and half-melted snow, and on all sides you hear the drip of falling moisture and the ripple of little streams of water which are running away to swell the creeks and rivers in every valley bottom.

You are shockingly unsteady on your feet, and feel very dazed and feeble; but you are also hungrier than ever now, with the keen morning air whetting your appetite, and the immediate business ahead of you is to find food. So you turn to the bank at your side and begin to grub; and as you grub you wander on, eating the roots that you scratch up and the young shoots of plants that are appearing here and there. And all the time the day is growing, and the sensation is coming back to your limbs, and your hunger is getting satisfied, and you are wider and wider awake. And, thoroughly interested in what you are about, before you are aware of it, you are fairly started on another year of life.

That is how a bear begins each spring. It may be a few days later or a few days earlier when one comes out; but the sensations are the same. You are always just as stiff, and the smells are as pungent, and the light is as strong, and the hunger as great. For the first few days you really think of nothing but of finding enough to eat. As soon as you have eaten, and eaten until you think you are satisfied, you are hungry again; and so you wander round looking for food, and going back to your den to sleep.

That spring when I came out it was very much as it had been the spring before, when I was a little cub. The squirrels were chattering in the trees (I wondered whether old Blacky had been burned in the fire), and the woodpecker was as busy as ever--rat-tat-tat-tat! rat-tat-tat-tat!--overhead. There were several woodchucks--fat, waddling things--living in the same gully with me, and they had been abroad for some days when I woke up. On my way down to the stream on that first morning, I found a porcupine in my path, but did not stop to slap it. By the river's bank the little brown-coated minks were hunting among the grass, and by the dam the beavers were hard at work protecting and strengthening their house against the spring floods, which were already rising.

It was only a couple of hundred yards or so from my den to the stream, and for the first few days I hardly went farther than that. But it was impossible that I should not all the time--that is, as soon as I could think of anything except my hunger--be contrasting this spring with the spring before, when Kahwa and I had played about the rock and the cedar-trees, and I had tumbled down the hill. And the more I thought of it, the less I liked being alone. And my father and mother, I knew, must be somewhere close by me--for I presumed they had spent the winter in the spot that they had chosen--so I made up my mind to go and join them again.

It was in the early evening that I went, about a week after I had come out of my winter-quarters, and I had no trouble in finding the place; but when I did find it I also found things that I did not expect.

"Surely," I said to myself as I came near, "that is little Kahwa's voice!" There could be no doubt of it. She was squealing just as she used to do when she tried to pull me away from the rock by my hind-foot. So I hurried on to see what it could mean, and suddenly the truth dawned upon me.

My parents had two new children. I had never thought of that possibility. I heard my mother's voice warning the cubs that someone was coming, and as I appeared the young ones ran and smuggled up to her, and stared at me as if I was a stranger and they were afraid of me, as I suppose they were. It made me feel awkward, and almost as if my mother was a stranger, too; but after standing still a little time and watching them I walked up. Mother met me kindly and the cubs kept behind her and out of the way. I spoke to mother and rubbed noses with her, and told her that I was glad to see her. She evidently thought well of me, and I was rather surprised, when standing beside her, to find that she was not nearly so much bigger than I as I had supposed.

But before I had been there more than a minute mother gave me warning that father was coming, and, turning, I saw him walking down the hillside towards us. He saw me at the same time, and stopped and growled. At first, I think, not knowing who I was, he was astonished to see my mother talking to a strange bear. When he did recognize me, however, I might still have been a stranger, for any friendliness that he showed. He sat up on his haunches and growled, and then came on slowly, swinging his head, and obviously not at all disposed to welcome me. Again I was surprised, to see that he was not as big as I had thought, and for a moment wild ideas of fighting him, if that was what he wanted, came into my head. I wished to stay with mother, and even though he was my father, I did not see why I should go away alone and leave her. But, tall though I was getting, I had not anything like my father's weight, and, however bitterly I might wish to rebel, rebellion was useless. Besides, my mother, though she was kind to me, would undoubtedly have taken my father's part, as it was right that she should do.

So I moved slowly away as my father came up, and as I did so even the little cubs growled at me, siding, of course, with their father against the stranger whom they had never seen. Father did not try to attack me, but walked up to mother and began licking her, to show that she belonged to him. I disliked going away, and thought that perhaps he would relent; but when I sat down, as if I was intending to stay, he growled and told me that I was not wanted.

I ought by this time to have grown accustomed to being alone, and to have been incapable of letting myself be made miserable by a snub, even from my father. But I was not; I was wretched. I do not think that even on the first night after Kahwa was caught, or on that morning when I saw her dead, that I felt as completely forlorn as I did that day when I turned away from my mother, and went down the mountain-side back to my own place alone. The squirrels chattered at me, and the woodpecker rat-tat-tat-ed, and the woodchuck scurried away, and I hated them all. What company were they to me? I was lonely, and I craved the companionship of my own kind.

But it was to be a long time before I found it. I was now a solitary bear, with my own life to live and my own way to make in the world, with no one to look to for guidance and no one to help me if I needed help; but many regarded me as an enemy, and would have rejoiced if I were killed.

In those first days I thought of the surly solitary bear who had taken our home while we were away, and whom I had vowed some day to punish; and I began to understand in some measure why he was so bad-tempered. If we had met then, I almost believe I would have tried to make friends with him.

I have said that many animals would have rejoiced had I been killed. This is not because bears are the enemies of other wild things, for we really kill very little except beetles and other insects, frogs and lizards, and little things like mice and chipmunks. We are not as the wolves, the coyotes, the pumas, or the weasels, which live on the lives of other animals, and which every other thing in the woods regards as its sworn foe. Still, smaller animals are mostly afraid of us, and the carcass of a dead bear means a feast for a number of hungry things. If a bear cannot defend his own life, he will have no friends to do it for him; and while, as I have said before, a full-grown bear in the mountains has no need to fear any living thing, man always excepted, in stand-up fight, it is none the less necessary to be always on one's guard.

In my case fear had nothing to do with my hatred of loneliness. Even the thought of man himself gave me no uneasiness. I was sure that no human beings were as yet within many miles of my home, and I knew that I should always have abundant warning of their coming. Moreover, I already knew man. He was not to me the thing of terror and mystery that he had been a year ago, or that he still was to most of the forest folk. I had cause enough, it is true, to know how dangerous and how savagely cruel he was, and for that I hated him. But I had also seen enough of him to have a contempt for his blindness and his lack of the sense of scent. Had I not again and again, when in the town, dodged round the corner of a building, and waited while he passed a few yards away, or stood immovable in the dark shadow of a building, and looked straight at him while he went by utterly unconscious that I was near? Nothing could live in the forest for a week with no more eyesight, scent, or hearing than a man possesses, and without his thunder-stick he would be as helpless as a lame deer. All this I understood, and was not afraid that, if our paths should cross again, I should not be well able to take care of myself.

But while there was no fear added to my loneliness, the loneliness itself was bad enough. Having none to provide for except myself, I had no difficulty in finding food. For the first few weeks, I think, I did nothing but wander aimlessly about and sleep, still using my winter den for that purpose. As the summer came on, however, I began to rove, roaming usually along the streams, and sleeping there in the cool herbage by the water's edge during the heat of the day. My chief pleasure, I think, was in fishing, and I was glad my mother had shown me how to do it. No bear, when hungry, could afford to fish for his food, for it takes too long; but I had all my time to myself, and nearly every morning and evening I used to get my trout for breakfast or for supper. At the end of a long, hot day, I know nothing pleasanter than, after lying a while in the cold running water, to stretch one's self out along the river's edge, under the shadow of a bush, and wait, paw in water, till the trout come gliding within striking distance; and then the sudden stroke, and afterwards the comfortable meal off the cool juicy fish in the soft night air. I became very skilful at fishing, and, from days and days of practice, it was seldom indeed that I lost my fish if once I struck.

Time, too, I had for honey-hunting, but I was never sure that it was worth the trouble and pain. In nine cases out of ten the honey was too deeply buried in a tree for me to be able to reach it, and in trying I was certain to get well stung for my pains. Once in a while, however, I came across a comb that was easy to reach, and the chance of one of those occasional finds made me spend, not hours only, but whole days at a time, looking for the bees' nests.

Along by the streams were many blueberry-patches, though none so large as that which had cost Kahwa her life; but during the season I could always find berries enough. And so, fishing and bee-hunting, eating berries and digging for roots, I wandered on all through the summer. I had no one place that I could think of as a home more than any other. I preferred not to stay near my father and mother, and so let myself wander, heading for the most part westward, and farther into the mountains as the summer grew, and then in the autumn turning south again. I must have wandered over many hundred miles of mountain, but when the returning chill in the air told me that winter was not very far away, I worked round so as to get back into somewhat the same neighborhood as I had been in last winter, no more, perhaps, than ten miles away.

On the whole, it was an uneventful year. Two or three times I met a grizzly, and always got out of the way as fast as I could. Once only I found myself in the neighborhood of man, and I gave him a wide berth. Many times, of course--in fact, nearly every day--I met other bears like myself, and sometimes I made friends with them, and stayed in their company for the better part of a day, perhaps at a berry-patch or in the wide shallows of a stream. But there was no place for me--a strong, growing he-bear, getting on for two years old--in any of the families that I came across. Parents with young cubs did not want me. Young bears in their second year were usually in couples. The solitary bears that I met were generally older than I, and, though we were friendly on meeting, neither cared for the other's companionship. Again and again in these meetings I was struck by the fact, that I was unusually big and strong for my age, the result, I suppose, as I have already said, of the accident that threw me on my own resources so young. I never met young bears of my own age that did not seem like cubs to me. Many times I came across bears who were one and even two years older than myself, but who had certainly no advantage of me in height, and, I think, none in weight. But I had no occasion to test my strength in earnest that summer, and when winter came, and the mountainpeaks in the neighborhood showed white again against the dull gray sky, I was still a solitary animal, and acutely conscious of my loneliness.

That year I made my den in a cave which I found high up on a mountain-side, and which had evidently been used by bears at some time or other, though not for the last year or two. There I made my nest with less trouble than the year before, and at the first serious snowfall I shut myself up for another long sleep.

CHAPTER IX.

I FIND A COMPANION.

The next spring was late. We had a return of cold weather long after winter ought to have been over, and for a month or more after I moved out it was no easy matter to find food enough. The snow had been unusually deep, and had only half melted when the cold returned, so that the remaining half stayed on the ground a long while, and sometimes it took me all my time, grubbing up camas roots, turning over stones and logs, and ripping the bark off fallen trees, to find enough to eat to keep me even moderately satisfied. Besides the mice and chipmunks which I caught, I was forced by hunger to dig woodchucks out of their holes, and eat the young ones, though hitherto I had never eaten any animal so large.

Somehow, in one way and another, I got along, and when spring really came I felt that I was a full-grown bear, and no longer a youngster who had to make way for his elders when he met them in the path. Nor was it long before I had an opportunity of seeing that other bears also regarded me no longer as a cub.

[Illustration: TOLD ME BLUNTLY THAT I MUST GO.]

I had found a bees' nest about ten feet up in a big tree, and of course climbed up to it; but it was one of those cases of which I have spoken, when the game was not worth the trouble. The nest was in a cleft in the tree too narrow for me to get my arm into, and I could smell the honey a foot or so away from my nose without being able to reach it--than which I know nothing more tantalizing. And while you are hanging on to a tree with three paws, and trying to squeeze the fourth into a hole, the bees have you most unpleasantly at their mercy. I was horribly stung about my face, both my eyes and my nose were smarting abominably, and at last I could stand it no longer, but slid down to the ground again.

When I reached the ground, there was another bear standing a few yards away looking at me. He had a perfect right to look at me, and he was doing me no sort of harm; but the stings of the bees made me furious, and I think I was glad to have anybody or anything to vent my wrath upon. So as soon as I saw the other bear I charged him. He was an older bear than I, and about my size; and, as it was the first real fight that I had ever had, he probably had more experience. But I had the advantage of being thoroughly angry and wanting to hurt someone, without caring whether I was hurt myself or not, while he was feeling entirely peaceable, and not in the least anxious to hurt me or anybody else. The consequence was that the impetuosity of my first rush was more than he could stand. Of course he was up to meet me, and I expect that under my coat my skin on the left shoulder still carries the marks of his claws where he caught me as we came together.

But I was simply not to be denied, and, while my first blow must have almost broken his neck, in less than a minute I had him rolling over and over and yelling for mercy. I really believe that, if he had not managed to get to his feet, and then taken to his heels as fast as he could, I would have killed him. Meanwhile the bees were having fun with us both.

It was no use, however angry I might be, to stop to try and fight them; so soon as the other bear had escaped I made my own way as fast as I could out of the reach of their stings, and down to the stream to cool my smarting face. As I lay in the water, I remember looking back with astonishment to the whole proceeding. Five minutes before I had had no intention of fighting anybody, and had had no reason whatever for fighting that particular bear. Had I met him in the ordinary way, we should have been friendly, and I am not at all sure that, if I had had to make up my mind to it in cold blood, I should have dared to stand up to him, unless something very important depended on it. Yet all of a sudden the thing had happened. I had had my first serious fight with a bear older than myself, and had beaten him. Moreover, I had learned the enormous advantage of being the aggressor in a fight, and of throwing yourself into it with your whole soul. As it was, though I was astonished at the entire affair and surprised at myself, and although the bee-stings still hurt horribly, I was pretty well satisfied and rather proud.

Perhaps it was as well that I had that fight then, for the time was not far distant when I was to go through the fight of my life. A bear may have much fighting in the course of his existence, or he may have comparatively little, depending chiefly on his own disposition; but at least once he is sure to have one fight on which almost the whole course of his life depends. And that is when he fights for his wife. Of course he may be beaten, and then he has to try again. Some bears never succeed in winning a wife at all. Some may win one and then have her taken from them, and have to seek another; but I do not believe that any bear chooses to live alone. Every one will once at least make an effort to win a companion. The crisis came with me that summer, though many bears, I believe, prefer to run alone until a year, or even two years, later.

The summer had passed like the former one, rather uneventfully after the episode of the bees. I wandered abroad, roaming over a wide tract of country, fishing, honey-hunting, and finding my share of roots and beetles and berries, sheltering during the heat of the day, and going wherever I felt inclined in the cool of the night and morning. I think I was disposed to be rather surly and quarrelsome, and more than once took upon myself to dispute the path with other bears; but they always gave way to me, and I felt that I pretty well had the mountains and the forests for my own. But I was still lonely, and that summer I felt it more than ever.

The late spring had ruined a large part of the berry crop, and the consequence was that, wherever there was a patch with any fruit on it, bears were sure to find it out. There was one small sheltered patch which I knew, where the fruit had nearly all survived the frosts. I was there one evening, when, not far from me, out of the woods came another bear of about my size. I liked her the moment I obtained a good view of her. She saw me, and sat up and looked at me amicably.

I had never tried to make love before, but I knew what was the right thing to do; so I approached her slowly, walking sideways, rubbing my nose on the ground, and mumbling into the grass to tell her how much I admired her. She responded in the correct way, by rolling on the ground. So I continued to approach her, and I cannot have been more than five or six yards away, when out of the bushes behind her, to my astonishment, came a he-bear. He growled at me, and began to sniff around at the bushes, to show that he was entirely ready to fight if I wanted to. And of course I wanted to. I probably should have wanted to in any circumstances, but when the she-bear showed that she liked me better than him, by growling at him, I would not have gone away, without fighting for her, for all the berries and honey in the world. One of the most momentous crisis in my life had come, and, as all such things do, had come quite unexpectedly.

He was as much in earnest as I, and for a minute we sidled round growling over our shoulders, and each measuring the other. There was little to choose between us, for, if I was a shade the taller, he was a year older than I, and undoubtedly the heavier and thicker. In fighting all other animals except those of his kind, a bear's natural weapons are his paws, with one blow of which he can crush a small animal, and either stun or break the neck of a larger one. But he cannot do any one of these three things to another bear as big as himself, and only if one bear is markedly bigger than the other can he hope to reach his head, so as either to tear his face or give him such a blow as will daze him and render him incapable of going on fighting. A very much larger bear can beat down the smaller one's arms, and rain such a shower of blows upon him as will convince him at once that he is overmatched, and make him turn tail and run. When two are evenly matched, however, the first interchange of blows with the paws is not likely to have much effect either way, and the fight will have to be settled by closing, by the use of teeth and main strength. But, as I had learned in my fight that day when I had been stung by the bees, the moral effect of the first may be great, and it was in that that my slight advantage in height and reach was likely to be useful, whereas if we came to close quarters slowly the thicker and stockier animal would have the advantage. So I determined to force the fighting with all the fury that I could; and I did.

It was he who gave the first blow. As we sidled up close to one another, he let out at me wickedly with his left paw, a blow which, if it had caught me, would undoubtedly have torn off one of my ears. Most bears would have replied to that with a similar swinging blow when they got an opening, and the interchange of single blows at arms' length would have gone on indefinitely until one or the other lost his temper and closed. I did not wait for that. The instant the first blow whistled past my head I threw myself on my hindquarters and launched myself bodily at him, hitting as hard as I could and as fast, first with one paw and then with the other, without giving him time to recover his wits or get in a blow himself. I felt him giving way as the other bear had done, and when we closed he was on his back on the ground, and I was on the top of him.

The fight, however, had only begun. I had gained a certain moral effect by the ferocity of my attack, but a bear, when he is fighting in earnest, is not beaten by a single rush, nor, indeed, until he is absolutely unable to fight longer. Altogether we must have fought for over an hour. Two or three times we were compelled to stop and draw apart, because neither of us had strength left to use either claws or jaw. And each time when we closed again I followed the same tactics, rushing in and beating him down and doing my best to cow him before we gripped; and each time, I think, it had some effect--at least to the extent that it gave me a feeling of confidence, as if I was fighting a winning fight.

The deadliest grip that one bear can get on another is with his jaws across the other's muzzle, when he can crush the whole face in. Once he very nearly got me so, and this scar on the side of my nose is the mark of his tooth; but he just failed to close his jaws in time. And, as it proved then, it is a dangerous game to play, for it leaves you exposed if you miss your grip, and in this case it gave me the opportunity that I wanted, to get my teeth into his right paw just above the wrist. My teeth sank through the flesh and tendons and closed upon the bone. In time, if I could hold my grip, I would crush it. His only hope lay in being able to compel me to let go, by getting his teeth in behind my ear; and this we both knew, and it was my business with my right paw to keep his muzzle away.

A moment like that is terrible--and splendid. I have never found myself in his position, but I can imagine what it must be. We swayed and fell together, and rolled over and over--now he uppermost, and now I; but never for a second did I relax my hold. Whatever position we were in, my teeth were slowly grinding into the bone of his arm, and again and again I felt his teeth grating and slipping on my skull as I clawed and pushed blindly at his face to keep him away. More and more desperate he grew, and still I hung on; and while I clung to him in dead silence he was growling and snarling frantically, and I could hear his tone getting higher and higher till, just as I felt the bone giving between my teeth, the growling broke and changed to a whine, and I knew that I had won.

One more wrench with my teeth, and I felt his arm limp and useless in my mouth. Then I let go, and as he cowered back on three legs I reared up and fell upon him again, hitting blow after blow with my paws, buffeting, biting, beating, driving him before me. Even now he had fight left in him; but with all his pluck he was helpless with his crippled limb, and slowly I bore him back out of the open patch, where we had been fighting into the woods, and yard by yard up the hill, until at last it was useless for him to pretend to fight any longer, and he turned and, as best he could, limping on three legs, ran.

During the whole of the fight the she-bear had not said a word, but sat on the ground watching and awaiting the result. While the battle was going on I had no time to look at her; but in the intervals when we were taking breath, whenever I turned in her direction, she avoided my eye and pretended not to know that I was there or that anything that interested her was passing. She looked at the sky and the trees, and washed herself, or did whatever would best show her indifference. All of which only told me that she was not indifferent at all.

Now, when I came back to her, she still pretended not to see me until I was close up to her, and when I held out my nose to hers she growled as if a stranger had no right to behave in that way. But I knew she did not mean it; and I was very tired and sore, with blood running from me in a dozen places. So I walked a few yards away from her and lay down. In a minute she came over to me and rubbed her nose against mine, and told me how sorry she was for having snubbed me, and then began to lick my wounds.

As soon as I was fairly rested, we got up and made our way in the bright moonlight down to the river, so that I could wash the blood off myself and get the water into my wounds. We stayed there for a while, and then returned to the patch and made a supper off the berries, and later wandered into the woods side by side. She was very kind to me, and every caress and every loving thing she did or said was a delight. It was all so wonderfully new. And when at last we lay down under the stars, so that I could sleep after the strain that I had been through, and I knew that she was by me, and that when I woke up I should not be lonely any more, it all seemed almost too good to be true. It was as if I had suddenly come into a new world and I was a new bear.

THE END.